Adelaid
Domestic Crusader

by
Cheryl MacDonald

Dundurn Press
Toronto and Reading
1986

Design and Production: Andy Tong
Typesetting: Typografix Inc.
Printing and Binding: Heritage Publications,Peterborough, Ontario

The writing of this manuscript and the publication of this book were made possible by support from several sources. The author is grateful to The Ontario Arts Council for a Writer's Grant award, and the publisher wishes to acknowledge the generous assistance and ongoing support of **The Canada Council**, the **Book Publishing Development Programme** of the **Department of Communications** and **The Ontario Arts Council**.

Care has been taken to trace the ownership of copyright material used in the text (including the illustrations). The author and publisher welcome any information enabling them to rectify any reference or credit in subsequent editions.

J. Kirk Howard, Publisher

Dundurn Press Limited
1558 Queen Street East
Toronto, Ontario
M4L 1E8

Dundurn Distribution
Athol Brose, Wargrave
Reading, England
RG10 8D

Canadian Cataloguing in Publication Data

MacDonald, Cheryl, 1952-
   Adelaide Hoodless : domestic crusader

(Dundurn Lives)
Bibliography: p.
Includes index.
ISBN 1-55002-018-8 (bound). - ISBN 1-55002-017-X (pbk.)

1. Hoodless, Adelaide, 1857-1910. 2. Canada -
Biography. 3. Women - Canada - Social Conditions -
History. 4. Women - Canada - Societies and clubs -
History. 5. Home economics - Study and teaching -
Canada - History. I. Title. II. Series.

Adelaide Hoodless
Domestic Crusader

by
Cheryl MacDonald

Portrait of Adelaide Hoodless by J. W. L. Forster.

CONTENTS

Acknowledgements

No book is the work of one individual. There are always others who help through suggestions, directions, casual comments and other means. This book was no exception, and while it is impossible to mention everyone who offered help and encouragement, there are several people who warrant special mention. These include Kathleen Mathews and her staff in the Hamilton Public Library's Special Collections section, Joyce Lindsay and her staff at the Selkirk (City of Nanticoke) Public Library, Nancy Sadek and her staff at the University of Guelph's Archival Collection, and W. Glen Curnoe of the London Public Library. Members of various organizations also assisted, including Doug Ketterborn's staff at the Hamilton Board of Education, Margaret Wingfield, CBE, of Britain's National Council of Women, and Muriel Beatty and Pearl Dobson of the Canadian National Council; Nancy Dodsworth, curator of the Adelaide Hunter Hoodless Homestead in St. George, Bev Holloway of the Ontario Agricultural Museum, Milton and Ingrid Jenkner, Macdonald Stewart Art Centre, all helped in providing photographs. I must also express appreciation to members of the Media Club of Canada, Hamilton Branch, who kept their eyes and ears open for helpful information, and special thanks to Terry Crowley, who graciously allowed me access to his manuscript on Adelaide Hoodless. As always, thanks go to Kirk Howard, my publisher, and the Ontario Arts Council, and last, but not least, to my family, especially my daughter, Catherine Riley, who assisted in proofreading and indexing.

Dedication

For My Grandmother
Emily McGrory Millar
Who practiced what Adelaide Hoodless preached.

Foreword

Until 1977, when my husband and I moved to Ontario, I had never heard of Adelàide Hoodless. An historical plaque was my first encounter with both Adelaide and the Women's Institutes. Since then, I have come to know Adelaide well, and to learn that she is probably better known internationally than any other Canadian woman, living or dead.

I have also become increasingly aware of two schools of thought concerning Adelaide and her accomplishments. One, exemplified by the popular literature dealing with her life, portrays Adelaide Hoodless as a candidate for sainthood, a woman of upstanding character and determination who worked selflessly for the improvement of family life in Canada. The second, currently popular with academics and feminists, portrays Adelaide Hoodless as a sinner against the feminist cause, an ultra-conservative whose desire to maintain middle class standards of living did nothing to advance the women's movement.

In reading this book, Adelaide's most ardent supporters may be offended to learn of some of her less attractive characteristics. Feminists may be outraged at the reactionary ideas which Adelaide and many of her contemporaries accepted as progressive. But, whether her ideas and accomplishments were right or wrong, progressive or regressive (by the standards of the 1980s) is irrelevant. It is my contention that Adelaide was neither saint nor sinner. She was a Victorian woman with a great deal of energy and ambition, which she channeled into areas she felt were important. This book, the first full-length biography of Adelaide Hoodless, is an attempt to acquaint readers with the woman, her work, and the times in which she lived.

Hunter ~ Hoodless Family Tree

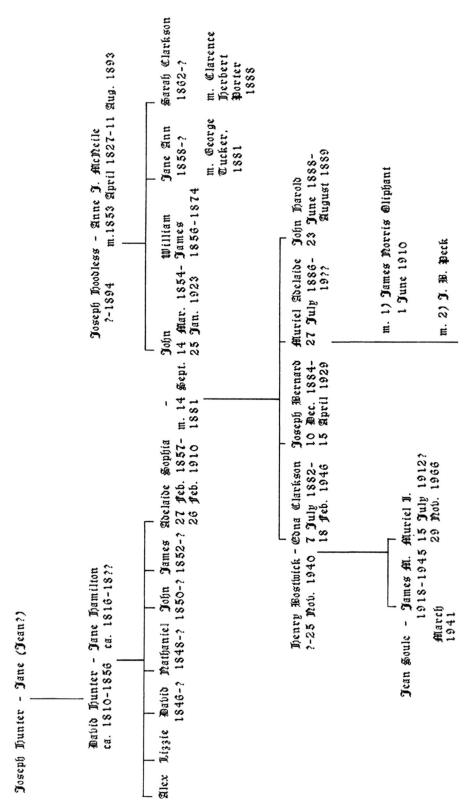

Chapter One

A Young Victorian Matron

Adelaide Hunter Hoodless is paradoxically one of the most famous Canadian women of the late Victorian era and one of the most obscure. More than forty thousand members of the Women's Institute recognize her as the founder of the organization, and through their international affiliations her name is known around the world. Two Ontario museums commemorate Adelaide and her accomplishments. Yet only the vaguest impressions of her formidable personality remain, and the nearly superhuman energy she expended in creating her legacy has been largely forgotten.

What was her legacy? It was a product of Adelaide's time, refined by her own driving energy. At the end of the nineteenth century, many municipalities were extending the franchise to women. For most women, nevertheless, community involvement meant charitable works, usually centred around the church. Yet these same years saw more and more women entering male-dominated fields. Emily Stowe became Canada's first woman doctor; her daughter, Augusta Stowe Gullen, joined the staff of Ontario's first medical school for women. The first female lawyers and dentists set up practice and more and more women began to earn university degrees.

Most women did not go to these extremes, but many did support the progress other women made, for then, as is often the case now, women and children were the most pathetic victims of poverty and other social ills. Untrained for any but the most menial tasks, discouraged by social pressures from entering well-paying but male-dominated fields, they suffered in silence. Even those who met society's expectations by marrying faced a life of drudgery. Only the financially comfortable could afford servants, and even the servants came and went in rapid succession as maids and laundresses left to start families of their own.

The average woman shouldered the entire burden of running the home. And what a burden! Mechanical aids were a rarity. Women washed with scrub boards and wringers, irons might weigh five pounds, and there were no permanent-press fabrics. Cooking was a monumental task. Kitchens were poorly organized, and there were no convenience foods. The care of ailing children and husbands generally fell upon Mother, who dosed them with simple folk remedies which might or might not prove efficacious. Add to these conditions a widespread ignorance of nutrition and hygiene and it is little wonder that mortality rates were high, particularly among children under five and women of childbearing age.

It is to these appalling conditions that women like Adelaide Hoodless turned their attention. The list of organizations with which Adelaide was involved reflects her dedication to the welfare of women and their families. As she said on more than one occasion, ''A Nation cannot rise above the level of its homes.''[1] Because of this belief, she supported the work of a variety of organizations. She was a founding member of the Victorian Order of Nurses, an organization designed to bring medical care to people in outlying districts, or to those too poor to avoid conventional health care. She was active in both the national and international Councils of Women, which served as a forum for the interchange of ideas by countless women's groups in Canada and abroad. She established the Women's Institute to provide domestic and agricultural training for rural women. And these activities were all secondary to her main goal: the establishment of domestic science training in Canadian schools.

While some of the organizations formed during this period quickly faded away, all those groups Adelaide helped organize remain intact. Some, like the VON and YWCA are familiar to almost everyone. Others, like the Women's Institute, are unknown to huge segments of the population, and yet every year hundreds of women from around the world, from places as remote as Sri Lanka and New Zealand, visit the site of the first Women's Institute in Stoney Creek, Ontario, as well as Adelaide's birthplace near Brantford. Although her public career was brief, spanning just two decades, her memory and her work survive three-quarters of a century after her death, fitting tribute to the woman one newspaper described as ''one of the most widely known educationists in Canada.''[2] Paradoxically, Adelaide can be viewed as either an early feminist or one of the worst enemies the feminist movement ever had. During her lifetime, many saw her as an outspoken advocate of radical reform. The idea of domestic science education was relatively new, and therefore suspect, and the suspicion with which it was regarded extended to its proponents. Adelaide's membership in organizations such as the National Council of Women did little to allay the fears of conservative Victorians, who were convinced women engaged in public life would eventually destroy society.

By modern standards, Adelaide was highly conservative. In the view of many modern feminists, her emphasis on woman as homemaker and mother helped buttress the patriarchal status quo. By insisting that girls be trained to run homes and raise families, Adelaide helped put women in an occupational ghetto from which they are only now beginning to escape.

Adelaide repeatedly spoke of her dream of improving Canadian society by improving conditions in Canadian homes. If there were flaws in her vision, they were the result of her own limited experience. As the daughter of a farmer and the wife of a prosperous businessman, Adelaide simply could not see the need for women to work outside the home, except in unusual circumstances, and then only temporarily.

This is not to say that Adelaide considered women inferior to men. Within the home, Adelaide saw women carrying out a range of activities no less demanding than those handled by men in the workplace. She never suggested that women were unsuited to work outside the home. Instead, faced with overwhelming evidence that women spent (and still spend) a large part of their lives raising families and caring for their homes, she proposed to make them experts at these tasks.

When Adelaide was born, Canada stood on the threshold of a new era. The country was little more than a network of settlements, loosely connected by roads, rivers, and, in more progressive areas, the new-fangled railways. Even the larger cities were mere provincial towns when compared with those of Europe, and their residents were in the minority. Most people lived in the country or in small villages, farming or trading in much the same way their forefathers had done before them.

But there were changes in the air. The Industrial Revolution which had shaken Europe in the previous century had its effect on Canada as well. Already the groundwork was being laid for a new, united Canada and the technology it would need as it approached the twentieth century, technology which included electricity, the telephone, and a transcontinental railway. Aside from these technological changes, there would be profound changes in the way people thought about themselves and society. Because the latter part of the nineteenth century would see sweeping reforms in almost every area of social endeavour, any child born in that era had a good chance of living through changes his or her parents had never imagined.

One such child was Adelaide Sophia Hunter, born 27 February 1857 at "The Willows", a clapboard farmhouse on Blue Lake Road near the village of St. George, Ontario. Her mother, the former Jean Hamilton, was about forty at the time, and Addie, as the new baby was called, would be the last of her ten children. Several months earlier, Jean's husband David had died.

David Hunter was an Irish Protestant who emigrated from Monaghan with his parents, brothers and sister around 1836. The Hunters settled in the Derry West section of the Township of Toronto, but when David married he moved 45 miles further west to St. George. Here, in 1851, he bought "The Willows", and it was here that Addie spent her childhood.

The loss of a father and husband frequently meant major hardship for a family, but the Hunters were sufficiently secure to allow some of Addie's brothers to attend college. There was, of course, no question of any of the girls attending college, for the few Canadian women who managed to fight their way into institutions of higher learning were regarded as oddities. Addie spent her early school years at the "German School", as the schoolhouse a mile and a half away was called.

When Addie was a child, the industrialization which would move

Birthplace of Addie Hunter, near St. Geroge, Ontario. Now a museum, the Adelaide Hunter Hoodless Homestead.

thousands of Canadians from the country to towns and cities had barely begun. It was reasonable, therefore, to expect her life would be similar to her mother's. She would marry, raise a family, and help her husband run a farm. Thus, almost as soon as she could walk, Addie had her share of chores to tend to. Typically, the first such chore was feeding the chickens and gathering eggs. As she grew older, her mother and sisters trained her in other skills essential to a farm wife: sewing, cooking, preserving, home nursing, gardening, housekeeping, beekeeping, care of livestock and so on. Addie learned that a farm woman's life was busy, often exhausting, and frequently made difficult by the isolation and lack of labour-saving devices. Nevertheless, there was always time for fun, at picnics and socials, trips to town to buy needed supplies, school celebrations, and, of course, church. The Hunters, as staunch Presbyterians, considered it unthinkable to miss services on a Sunday, unless, of course, heavy snows made the roads impassable.

Addie quickly learned the value of education, too. It was something her family praised highly. "There was an atmosphere of intellectual curiosity" in the household, "and encouragement to explore the world of literature through books — this may help to explain the educational advantages enjoyed by some of the older boys."[3] Growing up as the youngest of a large and close-knit family, she developed a good deal of confidence in her own abilities. And, like many youngsters secure in the affection of a large family and many friends, she learned to get along with other people at an early age, a knack that was polished during her sojourn at Ladies' College, which she is said to have attended while living with her married sister, Lizzie, in Cainsville. By the time Addie had grown to womanhood, she was poised, well-mannered, and deeply interested in the world around her.

Inevitably, a good portion of her interest in the world focussed on young men. Women married as a matter of course, for those who did not were looked on with pity, and there were few careers open to them at any rate. So Addie likely had her share of beaux in her teenage years and as she entered her twenties. In the course of time she fell in love with one particular young man, John Hoodless of Hamilton.

Born on 14 March 1854, John was the eldest son of a prominent furniture manufacturer, Joseph Hoodless, who had emigrated to Canada from Cumberland, England. The elder Hoodless prospered in his adopted country, for which he displayed a fierce patriotism. In 1866, when Fenian raids threatened the security of Canada, Joseph Hoodless "shouldered his rifle and marched to the scene of the conflict."[4] A shrewd businessman who was dedicated to the concept of public duty, Joseph nevertheless shunned politics, an example his oldest child chose to emulate.

John, who at one time played cornet in a Hamilton regimental band, joined his father in the family business in 1871. His only brother, William would likely have followed, too, but William died in 1874 at the age of 18.

Hamilton was a relatively small city in the middle of the nineteenth century, and most socially prominent citizens knew one another, if only on sight. Their social relationship extended beyond the city, too, because of membership in various organizations. Like his father, John was a freemason, and through this affiliation met many other young men and their families. It is possible that these introductions led to a meeting with Addie. Both John and his father knew Benjamin Charlton, who had been mayor of Hamilton from 1872 to 1874. Benjamin's brother was Seth Charlton, and Seth was married to Addie's older sister Lizzie.

John's courtship of the dark-haired and vivacious Addie Hunter followed the prescribed pattern: they saw each other in the company of other couples, family members and friends, but never alone. Evidence suggests the courtship was a long one. An autograph book survives containing the following verse:

I've a great mind to write prose
For I've had a bat on the nose
Administered by Miss Addie [good]
When in company with Miss Nellie Wood

P.S. Written while the impression was still there as received at a picnic party, May 24, 1877, by your

Sincere Admirer
John Hoodless[5]

Apparently the "bat on the nose" did little to dampen John's admiration for Addie, and after a suitable interval, they became engaged.

From Addie's point of view, John was a marvelous catch. Not only was he young and popular, a solid citizen and up-and-coming pillar of the community, he was also financially well off. Still, his wealth probably had little bearing on Addie's acceptance of the marriage proposal. As she told her daughter Muriel in later years, "I'd rather ride in a wheelbarrow with a man I love than a yacht with one I didn't."[6]

That is not to say Addie didn't feel at least a twinge or two of premarital jitters. In fact, there was one problem serious enough to warrant discussion with her minister. "Here I am, a strong Presbyterian and a Whig, planning to marry a man who is not only an Anglican but a Tory," she explained. "What should I do?"

The clergyman wisely replied, "My dear, you can be a good Christian in any church, but stick to your politics."[7] Addie would follow that advice for the rest of her life.

Following a hot summer in which many crops were ruined because of a prolonged drought, Addie married John at Zion Church in Cainsville on 14 September 1881. The ceremony was performed by the Reverend William Cochrane and witnessed by Addie's brother James, John's sister

Sarah and two friends. In marrying John, Addie exchanged her rural existence for life in the city, but she would always remain in touch with her roots, and this would eventually lead to one of her most outstanding achievements.

When John Hoodless brought his bride to Hamilton, the city had a population of about 36,000. Incorporated in 1846, it had initially been considered a serious rival for Toronto as the most important city in the province, but an economic depression in the '50s helped put an end to such dreams of glory. Instead, Hamiltonians learned to take pride in their "ambitious little city" and its growing reputation as an industrial centre, the "Birmingham of Canada."

It was a pleasant place to live despite the presence of industry, as the *New York Times* reported.

> Hamilton is a beautiful town. It lies at the head of Burlington Bay, the extreme westerly point of Lake Ontario, in a charming basin, made by the abrupt falling off of the table land to the vast upper country beyond....This valley lies warm and sheltered, and with its gradual slope to the lake, to give it drainage, and its soil composed partially of the debris of the disintegrated mountain limestone above, is of wondrous fertility and fruitfulness. The town is scarcely twenty years old... and is the chief entrepo [*sic*] and commercial mart of the extensive upper country to the west. The position of the town cannot be equalled. Its upper quarter overlooks the lake and bay; the broad valleys of Dundas, some miles above; the neighbouring heights and beautifully picturesque lands stretching out for miles opposite. Just behind the town, and hundreds of feet above it, is the mountain which looks down upon the town itself, even away beyond Toronto and into the misty blue of its far eastern boundary.[8]

Like the rest of Canada, this little town was growing rapidly. Many of the newcomers were immigrants from England, Ireland and Scotland, and the poorer ones congregated in the north end of the city where there were frequent violent outbursts between Catholic and Protestant Irishmen. For the most part, however, the citizens managed to get along despite their differences. For example, in 1887, when the Church of the Ascension, which the Hoodlesses attended, was severely damaged by fire, the congregation of Temple Anshe Sholem immediately offered its synagogue for services until the church was rebuilt.

Hamiltonians were deeply interested in improving the appearance of the city and the services it offered. A water system was in place and, a few years after Addie's arrival in the city, the first electric lights were installed, despite criticism from some individuals who objected to the plans to "plant ugly posts and string dangerous wires"[9] along the north side of King Street. Although many of the more wealthy residents tended to settle away from the downtown core, two central markets helped bring all Hamiltonians together in one area, if only temporarily.

John and Adelaide (after her marriage she insisted on the more dignified version of her name, going so far as to write over "Addie" in the family Bible; she may also have altered her birth date from 1857 to 1858) settled down in rented accommodations at 69 Hughson Street South. The house was probably decorated in the latest style, with heavy draperies, thick carpets, and rich, dark woods, since it was a showplace for the family business as well as a home. During the first few years of her marriage Adelaide led a life similar to that of most of her contemporaries. She was active in the church, socialized with friends and business associates of John's and their families, and, of course, started a family of her own. On 7 July 1882, Edna Clarkson Hoodless was born, followed by Joseph Bernard on 10 December 1884, Muriel Adelaide, 27 July 1886, and John Harold on 23 June 1888.

Adelaide was a doting mother, spending much time looking after her children, although she was always able to rely on servants to care for them when social obligations required her to be away from home. She prided herself on her skill as a mother, feeling she was conversant with the latest theories in child care, and so it was a particularly bitter blow when tragedy struck in the summer of 1889. On Saturday, 10 August, the *Hamilton Spectator* ran a brief obituary. "Hoodless — at 55 East Avenue South, John Harold, youngest son of John and Adelaide Hoodless, aged 14 months. Funeral at 4 o'clock p.m. Saturday. Friends will please accept this intimation."[10]

Adelaide's baby is said to have died of summer complaint, an intestinal ailment caused by drinking contaminated milk. Every summer, dozens of babies succumbed to the illness, which was largely due to poor sanitation. Although Louis Pasteur had reported on bacteria years earlier, most people were relatively ignorant of the basic rules of hygiene. Milk was delivered in open containers in Hamilton, accessible to flies and other disease carriers. While there were attempts to control the quality of milk, some dairy farmers continued to feed their cows garbage and contaminated material, or pastured them in fields of raw sewage. Some middlemen who distributed the milk were worse yet, adding chemicals like saltpetre, boracic acid and baking soda to the milk to make it look fresher, thus ensuring sales.

Ironically, there is some evidence that the Hoodless family kept their own cow. By this time they were living on East Avenue South, surrounded by enough land to support a garden and a cow. Was the animal suffering from a disease that affected its milk? Had the milk gone bad because of improper handling? Or had the cow run dry, making it necessary for Adelaide to purchase milk? Whatever the case, Adelaide apparently blamed herself for the baby's death. For the rest of her life, she would be particularly sensitive to issues of domestic hygiene.

In the meantime she consoled herself with her other children, and, in her typical fashion, looked about for some outlet for her energy, some method of assuaging her grief and helping to prevent similar tragedies. She found her solution in a career of voluntary public service.

Adelaide, baby Muriel, Edna, Bernard, ca. 1887.

Chapter Two

Early Work with the YWCA

Adelaide was probably involved in some type of church work from the time she joined the congregation of the Church of the Ascension. It went without saying in the late 1880s that, if you were an upstanding member of the community, you attended church. In English Canada, that meant a Protestant church, preferably Anglican or at the very least Presbyterian, for, despite the prominence of such Methodists as Timothy Eaton and Egerton Ryerson, the established churches of England and Scotland were the churches of Canadian society.

While religion may have been a great comfort to the poor and the oppressed, it was also a serious matter to many of the wealthy and influential members of society. In January 1889, for instance, Hamilton police chief McKinnon started a campaign to enforce business closures on Sundays. Apparently devout citizens of the ambitious city were scandalized to learn that children were buying candy on their way to Sunday School! Another incident, which took place at the Church of the Ascension, demonstrates to what lengths Hamiltonians would go in matters of religion.

Located on John Street South between Charlton and Forest Avenues, the Church of the Ascension was begun in May 1850 and opened on 22 June 1851, with Bishop Strachan, the most prominent cleric in Upper Canada, preaching a sermon. After the disastrous fire of 1887, the church was rebuilt and opened once more on 4 March 1888. For a time things went smoothly, and then a schism developed with most of the congregation on one side and the minister and a few supporters on the other.

The minister, the Reverend Edward Patrick Crawford, had high church leanings. In contrast, most of the congregation were inclined to an evangelical form of religion without any of the "romish" trappings favoured by the minister. Despite repeated requests from the congregation, Mr. Crawford attempted to introduce romish innovations to the service. At one meeting in 1890 he was severely criticized. Infuriated, he declared the meeting illegal and left. John Hoodless stepped in and took the chair, and ultimately Mr. Crawford was asked to resign since he refused to change his approach to worship.

Mr. Crawford refused. For a time the congregation waited, hoping, perhaps, that the threat of losing his position would convince Mr. Crawford to mend his ways. It did not, so, at another meeting on 22 September 1891, John Hoodless moved that "no fuel be purchased for the use of the church or Sunday School." [1] The People's Warden was asked to have the gas company remove all meters from the building and to have the water supply cut off. If the congregation could not convince Mr. Crawford to leave peaceably, they would make it uncomfortable for him to remain. Eventually, he resigned, and a new minister (with the correct view of how the services ought to be conducted) was hired.

The incident demonstrates that John Hoodless was not afraid to take a public stand on matters of personal importance, and suggests that he was a man of integrity and competence. Both these qualities are important, in light of Adelaide's very public career, in which her husband was often overshadowed, and sometimes accused of being henpecked.

As a convert from Presbyterianism, Adelaide must have supported John's point of view on the subject of the services. Her part in the imbroglio would have been a small one, however, since women had little say in the operation of the church. Besides, by this time Adelaide was busy with other work. She had become active in the YWCA.

Today we think of the Young Women's Christian Association as primarily an athletic organization. However, the word "Christian" in the Association's name provides an important clue to its origins and early history.

In the middle of the nineteenth century, a spiritual and social reform began in Britain which later influenced Canada and the United States. In time, the reform would give rise to the philosophy of a social gospel, a movement which saw Christianity as an active, vital force for good. Many of its proponents were educated, influential and rich, and, inspired by their beliefs, took steps to improve living and working conditions for those less fortunate than themselves.

The Young Women's Christian Association evolved from two separate organizations. Mary Jane Kinnaird (later Lady Kinnaird) was concerned with the number of girls streaming into London to volunteer for service in the Crimea. Many of these girls came from good, decent families, and, in accordance with the social standards of the day, should have been chaperoned on what was, for many, their first visit to London. But it was not practical in many cases for a family member to stay in London while the fledgling nurses waited indefinitely for ships to carry them to the front lines, and few of these young women had family or friends with whom they could stay. Kinnaird sympathized with their plight and their families' concerns, and decided to open a nurses' home in Fitzroy Square. Although originally meant to accommodate nurses, in the first year of operation the home sheltered "21 governesses and matrons, etc.; 2 school-mistresses; 2 matrons of immigrant ships; 9 nurses from the east; 2 foreigners; 1 young person in training for a school mistress; 1 lady in distress." [2] There was an obvious need for this type of shelter.

The Nurses' Home was not only a place to eat and sleep: it became a social centre for young women in a strange city. A programme developed which included an employment bureau and lending library, Bible study, and tea every Sunday to allow the women to meet and socialize. In 1858, the organization was named the Young Women's Christian Association.

Nearly twenty years later, Mary Jane Kinnaird called on Emma Robarts. This genteel schoolteacher had begun prayer unions, organizations which helped genteel young women meet to pray for spiritual enlightenment and guidance in their daily lives. Mary Jane admired Emma's work tremendously, and, after some discussion, the women joined forces. Thus, the religious interests of prayer unions became an integrated part of the organization which would become the YWCA.

By this time, the Young Women's Christian Improvement Association had crossed the Atlantic. The first Canadian branch opened at Saint John, New Brunswick, in 1870, with the stated goal of ''mutual spiritual improvement of its members, systematic circulation of suitable religious literature, the regular visitation of the poor and suffering, the promotion, wherever and whenever possible, of the knowledge and love of Jesus Christ our Lord.'' [3] Other towns and cities across Canada followed suit, with Toronto and Hamilton both opening branches in 1873.

Two factors helped change the nature of the Association over the next twenty years. Immigration increased, with men and women from Britain and other parts of Europe seeking a new life in Canada. Many of the women were young, hardly more than girls, single, and eager to find work at anything that was available. In most cases, that meant menial jobs, for, while highly trained British emigrants often obtained excellent positions, the bulk of the new arrivals were unskilled, suited only for domestic service or farm work.

Few immigrant women went to the farms. There was more money to be made in the cities, despite long hours and appalling conditions both in the shops and factories and in the crowded quarters where new arrivals lived. In addition, there was much competition from farm women who had left their rural birthplaces to seek jobs, money, and excitement in the city. A minority of these women had training in teaching, nursing, stenography or other skills which enabled them to find good jobs. Like their immigrant sisters, the majority were unskilled.

So, despite high hopes, jobs were not easy to find. A girl newly arrived in a strange city needed a place to stay until she found work, and sometimes even after she found work, for there was plenty of prejudice against working women, and landlords would not always rent rooms to them. It was to this problem that the concerned ladies of Canada addressed themselves.

On 18 March 1889, one hundred Hamilton women attended a meeting at the YMCA parlour on King Street. After reviewing the plight of young working women of the city, they voted to open a house to serve as a shelter for them. A week later, a larger group of women met in the Y's lecture room to form the Young Women's Christian Association. Many of the Women's Christian Associations in other cities had taken the step as a result of the perceived needs of working women, so the Hamilton organization was merely following a trend. Within a very short time, the group purchased the former residence of Dr. Henwood on Main Street West. It was opened on May 20th, and eight girls immediately took up residence.

Mrs. James Watson, former president of the Women's Christian Association, served as the first president of the Hamilton YWCA. She was succeeded in 1890 by Adelaide, who tendered her resignation at the end of her first year in office. Possibly Adelaide made the decision to resign because of pressure at home. In 1890, Hoodless and Son had gone into receivership. It was something of a shock to the Hamilton business community, for, in reporting the firm's liabilities at about $35,000, one city newspaper commented, ''it was generally supposed that the firm was doing a large and profitable business.'' [4] The article went on to explain the reasons behind the financial problems. ''The firm has taken a number of large outside contracts and was unable to finance the business, so much money being locked up in costly stock in the retail store, which has been run at a loss for some time.'' [5]

It was a temporary problem, soon rectified, but a worrisome one, and Adelaide might have felt that, if she could not focus her undivided attention on the Association, she should offer her resignation. Alternatively, the resignation might have been a ploy to gauge the level of her personal popularity: throughout her career, Adelaide would resign from various committees and organizations, then allow herself to be persuaded to remain. At any rate, the resignation was refused, indicating how highly regarded she was. She would hold the position until 1902, one of the longest terms ever served by a YWCA president.

As one of Adelaide's daughters later recalled, ''Her first active interest was in the YWCA.'' [6] It would appear that Adelaide was very popular with the other women in the group. A charming woman with a knack for organization and time management, she outshone many of her colleagues at executive and committee meetings. There is some indication, however, that she was initially hesitant to speak in public. On 27 January 1892, the *Hamilton Spectator* reported on an anniversary meeting of the YWCA. John Hoodless chaired the meeting, explaining ''that he acted as a chairman not only in order to relieve Mrs. Hoodless of a task she was too nervous to undertake, but also because he wished to show his sympathy with the work of the Association.'' [7]

By this time, the Association had gone beyond serving as a shelter for working women and was helping them learn saleable skills, including bookkeeping, shorthand, and dressmaking. The YWCA also acted as an employment agency for domestic servants, since many of the girls who went to the Association were interested in obtaining such work. This was a subject which concerned most of the women who helped run the organization, as they all knew how hard it was to find good help. And so they listened with interest to remarks made by Mrs. John Harvey of Toronto.

As the *Times* reported it,

> Various examples were given to show the benefits derived by the servants who were members of this association, and these invariably turn out just as good servants as the others in the city. The association is not a place for patronage, but it is a place where help is received and is also given. Four-fifths of the girls in Toronto who fall away from virtue are the very ones who are helpers in our households. The reason for this is that they are isolated from the household. She also said that it was the intention to try and have the servants work only eight or ten hours a day, instead of fifteen hours a day. [8]

The notion of reduced work hours must have shocked some of Mrs. Harvey's listeners and those who read the newspaper report. Then again, they may have expected to be shocked, for the YWCA was battling a good deal of prejudice, especially when it came to helping young girls from middle class homes to find work as stenographers or bookkeepers. As one report of the Ottawa Association wryly remarked,

> According to the popular notion, a lady may crochet the mat for a lamp to stand on but she may not clean the lamp. The line seems to have been drawn between work that is useful and work that is useless, the former being regarded as degrading while the latter is considered quite in keeping with the position of a lady. This false sentiment the Association seeks to remove in giving labour its true dignity, by including in its work those branches which enable young women to become true housewives and workers. [9]

Part of the work of the YWCA was to introduce new ideas to its membership, both to the young women who were members of the organization and the society matrons who ran it. So the Y frequently presented interesting speakers, such as Miss Laura Giddings, who talked on physical culture and dress reform in Hamilton on Saturday, 9 April 1892. The tall, slim brunette explained the need for good posture and physical fitness, then went on to talk about the problems of contemporary dress.

> I am a warm advocate for dress reform for women, and naturally I am the sworn enemy of the corset. Those steels which run up the centre of all corsets are the deadliest instruments of torture ever invented. The corset presses on the vital organs to such an extent that it is really a wonder that women can stand the torture. Candidly speaking I don't think that the good derived from my visit to Toronto by the ladies in my classes should have been ascribed to my system of teaching as much as to the fact that I persuaded so many of them to discard their corsets. The tendency of the corset is to thrust the abdomen forward and shoulders back, and in time makes the wearer altogether dependent on this artificial support.... Some people wear them because they are stout. Well, you know if compressed at one point the flesh has got to bulge out somewhere else, so that corsets do not make women a bit smaller. [10]

While some of Miss Giddings' more conservative listeners probably considered this plea to dispense with corsets just another fad, others listened carefully. There were changes in the air for women, an electric excitement they experienced as they came into contact with marvelous new ideas put forth by other women who were expanding the horizons of their sex.

The term "women's liberation movement" belongs to this century, but, in effect, there was a liberation movement underway in the late 1880s. In England, the United States and Canada, temperance and suffrage organizations worked toward a vote for women, and in some areas they achieved their goal. When Florence Nightingale went into nursing decades earlier, nurses were looked down upon, with some justification, since many of those who worked in hospitals were drunkards or prostitutes. By the 1880s, nursing had been raised to the status of a profession, and women didn't stop there. Instead, they entered universities, and a few persistent ones went on to become doctors and lawyers. These highly educated women were eager to have other women follow in their footsteps and frequently spoke to groups such as the YWCA. Adelaide could not help but be influenced by these new and dramatic changes in Canadian society, particularly after 1893, for, in May of that year, she was one of sixty Canadian women delegates to the International Congress of Women at the Chicago World's Fair.

Chapter Three

Council of Women

On Columbus day, 12 October 1892, six hundred and eighty-six acres along Lake Michigan were dedicated as the site of the World's Columbian Exposition. Although the fair ostensibly celebrated the four-hundredth anniversary of the founding of America, when it opened on 1 May 1893 it looked as much to the future as to the past.

While a host of foreign and native dignitaries, including the only living descendant of Christopher Columbus, looked on, US president Grover Cleveland pressed a button that illuminated thousands of electric lights and officially opened the fair. More than 27 million people would visit the site during the next six months, and most came away suitably impressed, for there was plenty to do and see in the carefully landscaped grounds. Visitors could gape at Eskimos or the scandalously exotic gyrations of Little Egypt. They might tour a Persian harem, visit a chamber of horrors, ride a camel through a re-creation of old Cairo. There was music to stir the emotions — the marches of John Phillip Sousa, conducted by Sousa himself, or the strains of the popular waltz, *After the Ball*. And, if the visitors grew weary of the myriad sights and sounds, they could refresh themselves at the Algerian cafe or any of the other fairground restaurants.

For thrill seekers, there was a moving pier that stretched out into the lake, and, wonder of wonders, the first Ferris Wheel. Designed by George W. Ferris, it loomed 280 feet above the ground and its 36 cars could hold forty passengers each.

The exposition offered much more than amusements and refreshments, however. Many countries had erected permanent buildings on the site, and some of the structures would have a profound influence on American architecture in the coming years. For those interested in culture, the works of such notable artists as Renoir, Whistler, and Sargent were on display. And a series of congresses on such subjects as history, science, religion, and literature kept visitors informed of the most modern trends of thought in the Victorian world.

Women played an important part in that Victorian world, for they were just beginning to wield their influence for public good. And so it was natural that this most modern of world fairs should include a most modern feature: the International Congress of Women.

The underlying idea of the Congress was to bring women together from around the world to exchange information and discuss their concerns. Scores of organizations were invited, including six from Canada, seven from France, thirty from England and fifty-six from the United States. Beginning at 11 a.m. on May 15th, the Congress ran until the evening of 21 May and encompassed seventy-six sessions. More than 600 women participated, and well over 150,000 women and men attended.

Stories on the World's Fair were carried in newspapers throughout Canada and the United States. On 3 May 1893, the *Hamilton Spectator* reported, "The Canadian Young Women's Christian Associations will be represented at the World's Congress of Women at Chicago by Mrs. John Hoodless of Hamilton, Mrs. Fairbairn of Peterboro, and Mrs. Harvie of Toronto."[1] As a member of the Canadian YWCA delegation, Adelaide naturally attended the sessions in which the organization was involved, but she must have also found time to attend others. The choice of which sessions to attend would not have been an easy one, for not only were the subjects under discussion intriguing, but the delegates were among the most notable women of the time. Jane Addams, founder of Hull House (Chicago's pioneer settlement house), was present, as was American Red Cross founder Clara Barton, and birth control crusader Margaret Sangster. Feminist Susan B. Anthony was in attendance; so were Dr. Emily Howard Stowe and her daughter, Dr. Augusta Stowe Gullen.

The YWCA sessions took place on 15 May. The Canadian delegation was headed by Mrs. Emily Cummings of Toronto, and among the topics discussed were, "The Association Working With The Church", "The Strength of the YWCA", and "The YWCA, its Methods and its Aims." Mrs. Harvie spoke on "What the Association does for Young Women", and it was she who communicated the feeling of sisterhood which permeated the Congress. A handsome woman with a prominent cleft chin, deep-set eyes and dark hair carefully parted in the centre, she said, 'As Canadian women we scarcely feel like foreigners, but know that we have much in common with our American sisters. We proudly boast the same noble ancestry." [2] That comment must have drawn appreciative nods from the many British women in attendance, and it likely echoed Adelaide's own feelings. In later years, her work would take her across the Canadian-American border so often it might as well not have existed.

Certainly Adelaide must have been drawn to the sessions on household economics and education, subjects in which she was already interested. The former was sponsored by the National Columbian Household Economic Association and aimed at informing women on the latest mesthods of running a household, including the employment of servants. If Adelaide had not yet completely formed her opinions on education, what she heard at the exposition must have influenced her to some extent. Kate Tupper Galpin discussed the "Ethical Influence of Education", a theme which would run through many of Adelaide's later talks. Said Galpin, "I believe it is important that a child be taught to drive nails, but it is of infinitely greater importance that he be taught to drive every nail that it is his duty to drive after he learns to drive nails. Attention, industry, promptitude and dispatch are much more difficult things to teach than Sloyd."[3] (Sloyd, a

Swedish word, referred to manual training, especially woodworking.)

Attention, industry, promptitude — all synonymous with duty, a concept with which Adelaide was intimately familiar. Duty to home, to family, to the church, to the community, had been a part of her life since infancy. In Chicago, she had the opportunity to hear how other women felt about these concepts. She was a member of the conference committee on religion, for instance, and she undoubtedly listened to speeches on education. With daughters of her own, she could not fail to be impressed by the remarks of Professor Ellen Hayes of Wellesley College.

> The girl who enters upon life in 1900 is going to have a fairer chance than her grandmother's mother had; and who is not glad to think of that woman of the far-off future in whose coming the analogies of science permit us to believe? In larger measure than any that we have experienced of, she will possess the truth, and truth will make her free. She will demand a knowledge of her own body, and how it is to be preserved in health and long life, a knowledge of the earth on which she lives and how to manage her living so that the forces of nature shall work for her; a knowledge of the social and political commonwealth, in which she is to be a unit, not a fraction, as is the case with her sister of today; a knowledge also of her social and political environment, viewed as a long result of time, connected with causes which have their beginnings in the animal life whence we came. On the intellectual side of her nature she will accept evidence or proof as a directive force in place of the now dominant emotions. On the aesthetic side she will realize that a home should not be a bric-a-brac shop, and that a woman gives in attention to the adornment of her person she loses in power to see and appreciate the splendour of the the wide world around her. [4]

With so many prophesizing a glorious future for womankind, Chicago was an exciting place to be. The very atmosphere was electric with the spirit of reform and Adelaide, already conscious of the problems facing both working women and homemakers, was stirred by the glimpses of what might be.

One of the more influential groups at the Congress was the International Council of Women. Two of the moving spirits behind the organization were Susan B. Anthony and Elizabeth Cady Stanton, who had toured England and France together, talking to women about their concerns. At a farewell reception in Liverpool in 1882, someone suggested the idea of a worldwide association in which organized women from various countries could participate. Six years later, the International Council of Women was founded at the Opera House in Washington, D.C., during a meeting attended by women from the United States, Canada, France, Scandinavia, and England.

Between 1888 and 1893, Clara Barton served as Director of the United States section of the International Council of Women, and, during those years the Council was largely dominated by American women, who arranged for the meeting of the Council in conjunction with the Columbian Exposition. At the conference, the delegates pledged to work towards the establishment of national councils in their respective countries, and, at the same time, Adelaide became deeply involved in the Council's work, for she was elected president of the Canadian section of the international council.

This affiliation of organized women was a concept that caught the imagination of many of the women who visited Chicago that May, especially the Canadian women. As Adelaide would explain,

> Canada was about the only country — representing advanced civilization — not officially represented through an official body of women, and, after hearing the reports of the various delegates and the influence exercised upon such municipal and legislative powers as exist in France, Germany, Denmark, Greece, Sweden, Great Britain, Australia and others in the short time they have been organized, besides affording an opportunity through the international meetings held every five years of learning what the women of other countries are doing, the advantages of such an organization was clearly demonstrated. There were only five Canadian organizations officially represented at the Congress, by the Dominion Women's Christian Temperance Union, the Young Women's Christian Association, the Missionary Society of Canada, the Dominion Order of King's Daughters and the Women's Enfranchisement Association. You will readily see how unfairly Canadian work was represented, and in order to prevent a repetition of such mistakes the Canadian delegates called a meeting then and there to discuss the question of forming a National Council for Canada. Each of the above mentioned societies had three delegates present, which were supplemented by several Canadian women who were attending the Congress, making in all about twenty-two in attendance. [5]

The result of their deliberation was the election of provisional officers who would undertake to form a National Council. As the women separated and returned to their homes throughout Canada, the United States and Europe, they carried with them memories of shared experiences and common concerns. Many were filled with enthusiasm for the projects that had been discussed, and, at the same time, were eager to keep in touch with the women they had met, despite the geographical distance between them. Undoubtedly, as their train chugged homeward, Adelaide and the other members of the Canadian delegation reviewed what they had heard and how it could be applied to their situation. Inevitably, talk turned to what action could be taken, and one of the results was a decision to make the YWCA a national organization.

Adelaide was back in Hamilton by May 25th. The next day, a new police magistrate was appointed, and, to mark the occasion Adelaide and several other women, including members of the YWCA, the Ladies' Benevolent Society, the YMCA Ladies Auxiliary, and the WCTU, signed a petition requesting the appointment of a police matron and protesting the sale of liquor to minors. The petition was presented to Police Magistrate Jelfs by Judge Muir, and duly reported in the local newspapers.

It was not unusual for women to draw up a petition and then have men present it. Women were frequently excluded from meetings of many organizations, and often had to rely on male champions to explain their requests to colleagues. Frequently, in fact, a cause would be lost if there was no male support for it, as women lacked power in a very real sense. It was only within their own organizations that they had any kind of power, and even here it was limited, because it did not often extend into the official male world. Women might organize to carry out charitable work, but they shouldn't concern themselves with reforms. Most reforms involved political action, something women — especially respectable women — were supposed to know nothing about. Politically-minded women and those whose wealth and position made them less vulnerable to ridicule tended to ignore these taboos and worked towards the reforms they considered necessary. But there was always some sense that, in carrying out their reforms, the women were engaged in something daring, although this changed slowly as more and more women were drawn to public action.

For Adelaide, one of the first major projects was the nationalization of the YWCA. She started this project immediately after her Chicago visit.

> Upon my return home I wrote to every city and town in Canada. When there were already established associations, I asked them for their views, etc. Where I did not know of any existing, I wrote the Mayor of the place asking for the information and if he would kindly place the letter in the hands of some responsible Christian woman who would assist me in my efforts to secure information. In all, I sent ninety letters; some were most courteously answered, others were ignored.[6]

It would take several weeks for the letters to reach their destinations and the replies to filter back to Hamilton. Unable to remain idle, Adelaide busied herself with various organizational and personal duties.

John, who had been on the Hamilton Board of Education for five years, was now chairman and frequently visited classrooms in the City's schools. When he did, Adelaide often accompanied him, gaining an insight into the education system which would prove useful before too long. In addition, the couple were planning to move to more luxurious accomodations at Eastcourt, a palatial house near present-day Main and Sherman Streets, which, in 1893, was beyond the eastern limits of Hamilton. (The house belonged to John's father, who preferred to live closer to downtown Hamilton and the family business.)

At the same time, both John and Adelaide led busy social lives. Adelaide enjoyed cards; she may also have liked sailing, for, when the Royal Hamilton

Yacht Club Beach House opened in May 1892 she was one of those in attendance. Her social life and her community service activities were inextricably linked, since many of the women with whom she played cards or dined were also members of local organizations. Because of this social interaction, and the fact that many women belonged to more than one group, members of one association were generally aware of what their counterparts were doing in other associations, at least within the same community. By the end of the summer of 1893, Adelaide was involved in plans to make these informal liasons formal and nationwide as a result of the establishment of the Canadian National Council of Women.

Adelaide's involvement with the Council led directly to an association with Ishbel, Lady Aberdeen, wife of the soon to be appointed Governor-General. Lady Aberdeen had attended various sessions at the Columbian Exposition. A dedicated, outspoken reformer, as well as a noted philanthropist, she impressed most of the women who heard her, and following the Congress of Women, her name was put forward as a candidate for new president of the International Council of Women.

By this time, Lady Aberdeen had returned to England, and, in fact, was unaware of the nomination. The executive of the International Council had decided that, since the next meeting was scheduled for London, a British woman should serve as president. Two names were suggested, those of Lady Henry Somerset and Lady Aberdeen. When the votes were counted, twelve members of the executive had voted for Lady Aberdeen, nine for Lady Somerset, and three had abstained.

Rachel Avery Foster telegraphed the news. ''You have been elected President of the International Council of Women. Writing.''[7] But, as she confessed in her memoirs, Lady Aberdeen had no recollection of the organization and cabled back, ''But what is the International Council of Women?'' A detailed letter explained the function of the Council, and, in response to further inquiries, said the president's chief duty would be to oversee the London Congress. It seemed largely an honorary position, so Lady Aberdeen accepted it and turned her attention to other matters, including the move to Canada where her husband was to take up his vice-regal duties. Still, as she later wrote, ''I was destined to be quickly educated as to what a National Council of Women might mean.''[8]

The groundwork for the National Council had been laid during the weeks following Adelaide's return from Chicago. In early October, two preliminary meetings were held in Toronto. On October 26th, Lady Aberdeen was in Hamilton for the unveiling of a statue of Sir John A. Macdonald, Canada's first prime minister, and apparently discussed the matter with Adelaide. A delegation from the YWCA was among those which greeted the vice-regal couple on their arrival in Hamilton, and, after the Association's secretary, Anna Helm, made a speech, Adelaide presented Lady Aberdeen with a bouquet of mauve chrysanthemums.

It is quite likely that this was not the first meeting between the two women. In 1890, the Aberdeens had lived briefly in Hamilton. In Chicago, as the future Governor-General's wife, Lady Aberdeen quite likely made a point of meeting most of the Canadian women involved in the Congress. Certainly there was ample time to make new acquaintances during the various social functions that punctuated the weeks's events. Did either woman suspect how closely their interests would coincide over the next several years?

Ishbel Maria Marjoribanks was born 15 March 1857, sixteen days after Addie Hunter. Certainly their similar ages helped draw the women together. But there were additional similarities: both had been raised as Presbyterians; both were devoted Liberals. Moreover, it is highly possible each recognized and admired in the other the energy and persistence necessary to accomplish the important reforms which would improve conditions for the women of Canada.

The day after the statue unveiling on 27 October, both women were in Toronto for the mass meeting which would inaugurate the National Council of Women. Fifteen hundred women attended the meeting at the Horticultural Pavilion, along with a handful of men. As the Toronto *Globe* noted,

> It was a meeting of women, for women managed by women — if exception be made of the part taken in it by the young men who acted as ushers, by the members of the orchestra and the policemen, and by Inspector James L. Hughes. With these exceptions the hand of masculinity was not visible, nor indeed was the need of it apparent. The prerogatives which they left to mankind were to find seats for them as the ushers did, to entertain their idle moments as the musicians did, to keep order for them as the policemen did, and to take up a collection for them as Mr. Hughes did, and even these they might have performed themselves if they had been of that mind. [9]

It was a fine autumn day, and this, coupled with curiosity about Lady Aberdeen, helped draw the largest crowd ever to attend a women's meeting in Toronto up to that time. Nearly every women's association was represented, and, as the *Globe* reporter pointed out, "It was an audience not of sharp-featured man-haters, denouncing mankind and scolding the course of civilization," [10] but of "pleasant-faced women" [11], many of them middle-aged representatives of "motherly womanliness." [12] In other words, in the view of the Victorian establishment, it was a highly respectable gathering.

Exactly how respectable it was can be judged from the list of women on the platform. Along with the Countess of Aberdeen were Adelaide and her YWCA associates, Mrs. Cummings and Mrs. Harvie, as well as Dr. Stowe Gullen, Lady Gzowski and more than a dozen other notable women from Toronto and elsewhere.

The meeting opened with Mrs. Mary McDonnell, the president of the provisional executive of the Women's Federation, as the Council had been called up to that time, reiterating the decision which had grown out of the

Chicago Congress, that a federation of Canadian women's organizations should be established. Then, after some introductory remarks and the presentation of a bouquet of flowers (the third she had received that day) Lady Aberdeen took the floor. As the glove-muffled applause subsided, she said how privileged she felt to be a part of the meeting:

> It is not the first meeting that I have attended having objects such as those which have been put before us. For, ladies, this happy movement towards unity between workers as distinguished from uniformity is in the air. We are beginning to realize that all the divisions we have put up between ourselves — the narrow grooves along which we accustom ourselves to run — our want of knowledge of one another's interest, one another's sympathies, one another's work, is keeping us back from fulfilling our life mission for God and humanity. And so, on both sides of the Atlantic, and in places far removed from each other, we can see in different ways a desire evinced that not only should workers having the same immediate aim unite together for that object, but that the various societies and associations should in their turn devise means whereby they may be brought into contact with one another. [13]

Lady Aberdeen spoke of the progress made by women's organizations over the past century, especially in the area of social reform. She also addressed the problem of rivalry between various women's associations, and told how a federation of women's societies in the United Kingdom was helping combat the problem. This federation, she said, was helping to awaken a deep sense of personal responsiblity in the women who attended its conferences. "If a sense of personal responsibility is awakened in any man or woman in an abiding way the battle is won," [14] she declared, and the audience broke out into applause.

> And do we women need especially to have that sense of responsibility continually deepened and intensified? We hear a great deal about women's influence — but do we believe it? Do we value our resonsibilities as mothers, as sisters, and friends, as the makers or marrers of home life, of social life? Do we believe in it as teachers, as guardians of the young, as those to whom it falls to mother those many motherless ones in this world of ours? What tremendous power is ours in all these ways![15]

She told how the conference held in England helped to educate and inform women, adding, "I believe that those who think that women's work for the public good unfit them for home life are profoundly mistaken," [16] a comment which again drew applause from the audience. "If undertaken in the right spirit, and only in such measure as will not interfere with the claims of home, I believe it should fit us to perform our home duties far more perfectly."[17]

As she concluded her speech, Lady Aberdeen said,

> I am requested to make the following motion: "Resolved: — that this meeting do heartily endorse the formation of a national council of women for Canada, believing that by means of such a federation a more intimate knowledge of one another's work will be gained, which will rely in large mutual sympathy, greater unity of thought, and therefore, in more effective actions, especially in matters that may arise from time to time which command a general interest."[18]

After the motion was seconded, the audience was asked to vote on it. Every woman in the room stood in support of the resolution, as did Inspector Hughes, President of the Toronto Women's Enfranchisement Association. Then a collection was taken up for the support of the new organization.

Before the meeting ended, an executive was elected, with Lady Aberdeen as president of the National Council of Women and Adelaide as treasurer. The first committee meeting was held the next day, followed by lunch at the Toronto YWCA.

Probably the best description of the organization's aims was given by Mary McDonnell, who became the Vice-President of the National Council:

> We, women of Canada, sincerely believing that the best good of our homes and nation will be advanced by our own greater unity of thought, sympathy, and purpose, and that an organized movement of women will best conserve the highest good of the family and the state, do hereby band ourselves together to further the application of the Golden Rule to society custom and law.[19]

The mention of the Golden Rule was a reference to the guiding principle of the Council, "do unto others as you would have them do unto you," a motto suggested by Lady Aberdeen which typified both the religiosity of the period and the prevailing spirit of social reform.

Despite the high-minded goals of the Council, there were several wrinkles to iron out before the members could concentrate on their various projects. One task was dispelling the impression that the Council was a political organization. The idea of political activity was still abhorrent to many of the women who belonged to the Council, although not to all. Certainly Lady Aberdeen was in favour of votes for women, although she took pains to reassure prospective members of the Council that it was not a suffrage organization.

Adelaide's attitude toward female suffrage was much more typical of her class and time, however. She was convinced that a woman's role was to influence her husband and sons to do good, and so there was no need for political power if she accomplished this goal. As late as October 1904, she would remark, "a woman who has not succeeded in training her sons to vote so that they will guard their mother's best interests and the best interests of the nation is not herself worthy to vote."[20]

A second problem was how to teach the member groups of the Council to work together towards common goals. Lady Aberdeen would write on how important and how difficult this task was. "...The idea of an organization simply designed to get all workers to know and appreciate one another, and to unite for common purposes has been difficult to inoculate, however it has been done."[21]

Finally, there was the problem of religious differences, specifically regarding what type of prayer should be used to open Council meetings. Given its fundamental purpose of uniting women in a common cause, it was essential that the organization not be fragmented by religious differences. Yet, as demonstrated by the fracas at Adelaide's own church, religious beliefs divided as often as they united. Following some discussion, which included the fact that Jewish women's organizations had expressed interest in the Council, the women decided that meetings should open with a silent prayer, thus satisfying their need for special guidance in their work without offending any members or stirring up religious prejudices.

Imagine the consternation of the women, then, when an Ottawa paper reported "National Council of Women Against Lord's Prayer."[22] This was the kind of irresponsible headline typical of many contemporary newspapers when reporting on women's organizations, and one of the tactics that helped create hostility towards such groups.

Yet, at the same time as some newspapers criticized women's organizations, others helped further their aims. One such publication was the *Toronto Empire*. "Hitherto it has not been the correct thing, from a Canadian society standpoint, for a woman to speak on a platform. But now, for the first time a Governor-General's wife has given a public address,"[23] the newspaper reported shortly after the Council was established. The paper went on to discuss the possibility that other women might follow suit, and surely Adelaide must have reflected on the influence woman could wield from the platform.

From its inception, the National Council of Women enjoyed a high profile, largely due to the prominence of many of its regular and honorary members. Lady Thompson, wife of Prime Minister Sir John Thompson, and Madam Laurier, wife of the future prime minister, were made vice-presidents at large, while wives of the provincial lieutenant-governors were made honorary vice-presidents. Its prominent membership, along with the energy and influence of its members, would result in the establishment of seven local councils of women within the next year, in Toronto, Montreal, Ottawa, London, Winnipeg, Quebec City, and Hamilton.

As an executive member of the National Council, Adelaide was instrumental in establishing the Local Council of Women in Hamilton. On 17 November 1893, the inaugural meeting was held in the Hamilton Board of Trade rooms, with Adelaide presiding, assisted by Mary McDonnell and Emily Cummings, both of Toronto. After Adelaide explained the origins of the Canadian National Council and how it had grown out of the Chicago

Exposition, Mrs. McDonnell reiterated the history of the American National Council. Then Adelaide passed around copies of the constitution of the national and local councils. One clause of the national constitution apparently drew particular interest, since it was later reproduced in the *Hamilton Times*:

> This council is organized in the interest of no one propaganda, and has no power over the organizations which constitute it beyond that of suggestion and sympathy: therefore, no society voting to enter this council shall render itself liable to be interfered with in respect to its complete organic unity, independence, or methods of work, or be committed to any principal method of any other society, or to any act or utterance of the council itself, beyond compliance with the terms of this constitution.[24]

Emily Cummings then drew attention to the objects of the National Council. To underline the importance of such an organization, she gave one example.

> She instanced the case of protests recently made by the women of British Columbia against the horrible practice of selling Chinese women which prevails along the coast with the full knowledge of the Dominion government. This protest was supported by all the Mission Boards having representatives in British Columbia, and a strong petition was sent to the Minister of Customs to have the law regarding the importation of Chinese women strictly enforced. The petition was pigeonholed in the Customs Department and no further notice taken of it. Now had such a protest emanated from a National Council of Women it would at least have been thought worthy of notice and might have been successful.[25]

Before the meeting ended, the officers of the Local Councils were elected. Mrs. J. R. Holden was president, Mrs. Adam Brown vice-president, Miss McKenzie, treasurer, Mrs. Woolverton, corresponding secretary, and Mrs. Reynolds, recording secretary. An executive meeting was scheduled for the following month.

Although Adelaide was not one of the officers elected to the Local Council, she continued to campaign for its success. At one point, she wrote a lengthy letter to the *Times*, describing the organization and its goals, and concluding with reference to opposition to the group.

> Being an entirely new feature in women's work in Canada, it has made those who have been working along their own special line view with suspicion any innovation in the way of a new organization for the purpose of federation, and as ''there is no one so blind as those who will not see,'' the task of its promoters has been no sinecure. In order to bring the matter more prominently before the women of Hamilton arrangements are being made for the President — that queen among women — Her Excellency Lady Aberdeen, to give an address on the subject in the near

future, and when one considers the opportunity thus provided for meeting and learning some of the charming qualities possessed by the Vice Regal Lady of Canada, and who has already won a place in the hearts of true women of the land such as none of her predecessors ever approached, this in itself is sufficient proof of the desirability of a National Council.... N. B. There are so many absurd ideas afloat concerning this organization that it will be a genuine act of kindness to publish the facts concerning it, and I assure you, it will be a matter of interest to newspaper reading women of the city. It makes the task so difficult for the officers, as no two people seem to have the same idea.... A. H.[26]

The newspaper obligingly published Adelaide's letter.

As 1893 drew to an end, Adelaide could look back on a year of challenge and change, if indeed there was any time for reflection. For, in the final weeks of the year, Adelaide was busily laying the groundwork for a national YWCA and an affiliated cooking school which would create a controversy with her firmly at its centre.

Eastcourt, the Hoodless family home, near Main and Sherman Streets, Hamilton, Ontario. Only the coachouse remains today.

Chapter Four

Cooking Classes at the YWCA

As 1894 approached, Adelaide busied herself with preparations for the holidays, her usual organizational duties, and the opening of cooking classes at the local YWCA. At the same time, she was nursing John through an illness. As the local newspapers reported, Hamiltonians were suffering from an outbreak of "la grippe." Consequently, on 15 December, John wrote to the Board of Education, explaining that he had a sore throat and could not attend a regular meeting. But the note was more than an apology for his absence: it was also a letter of resignation. The Hoodless's move to Eastcourt had taken them from Hamilton to Bartonville, so, as the Minister of Education informed him, since John was no longer a resident of Hamilton he was no longer eligible to sit on the Board of Education. Both the Board and the Hamilton newspapers expressed regret at John's enforced retirement, with the Board writing a letter of protest to the minister, asking that an exception be made in this case. Not only had John been a dedicated member of the Board for six years, he also— as *The Hamilton Times* pointed out — owned property in the city assessed at $30,000. But the Department of Education was adamant, and John reluctantly left the Board. In doing so, he averted the possibility of charges of nepotism and patronage which might have occurred had he retained his position during Adelaide's campaign for domestic science, although, at the time, neither he nor Adelaide would have looked upon the resignation as beneficial.

Yet Adelaide was already firmly set on the path which would lead her to repeated confrontation with the Board of Education. The YWCA had opened its cooking school, the first of its kind in the country. One of the first public indications of the plan was a report in the *Hamilton Spectator* on 2 January 1894, announcing the class would open later that month, and that a professional cook, Miss Surridge of Toronto, would teach.

The first class was held on schedule, on Saturday, January 20th, and reported upon by the *Hamilton Times*:

> At half past one, when the lecture began, upwards of thirty ladies with notebooks and pencils were ranged around the long kitchen table, whereupon were placed the various material required in the demonstrations. Miss Surridge was very ably assisted throughout by Mrs. Hoodless, Miss McKenzie and others. The ladies one and all declared the experiment a perfect success and the number will undoubtedly be doubled on Saturday next. Miss Surridge is a skilled professional and the beautifully ornamented cakes, dainty little Lavenue baskets,

feathery buns and other delicates found a ready sale at the close of the session.[1]

To understand why the opening of cooking classes was a newsworthy event, as well as one which provoked some controversy, it is necessary to understand the situation of Victorian women, especially popular attitudes towards women and work. While many women worked out of necessity, they were generally looked down upon. The workplace, with its coarseness and competitiveness, was no place for a woman. No, the proper sphere of the Victorian woman was the home, where she could exert her influence for good over the family. For middle class women in particular, it was not good enough to be a supportive wife, nurturing mother and good moral example. She must also be a skilled manager of the home, seeing to all the myriad of tasks essential to a family's comfort and to the demands of society.

There was a strong link in the minds of middle class Victorians between moral character and the efficient operation of the household. One expert explained,

> A clean, fresh and well ordered house exercises over its inmates a moral, no less than physical influence, and has a direct tendency to make members of the family sober, peaceable and considerate of the feelings and happiness of each other.[2]

Another writer warned of the results of shoddy housekeeping:

> There are numerous instances of worthy merchants and mechanics whose efforts are paralyzed, and their hopes chilled by the total failure of the wife in her sphere of duty; and who seek solace under their disappointment in the wine-party, or the late convivial supper. Many a day labourer, on his return at evening from his hard toil is repelled by the sight of a disorderly house and a comfortless supper... and he makes his escape to the grog-shop or the underground gambling room.[3]

To avoid driving her husband to the grog-shop or other unsavoury establishments, a Victorian wife was expected to perform a multitude of tasks, or supervise the servants who performed them. Yet, even if a woman was fortunate enough to be able to hire a domestic or two, there were certain jobs she handled herself as an indication of her skill as a homemaker. One of these was cooking.

In a time before convenience foods, electric or gas stoves, feeding a family was a complicated task. Keeping a wood stove at a constant temperature required a certain degree of skill, experience and knowledge of the burning qualitites of different types of wood. Furthermore, the selection and preparation of food was a formidable undertaking. Victorian meals were gargantuan by today's standards: a typical breakfast might include bread, cooked potatoes, fruit, beef, ham or fish. Almost all baked goods were made at home, generally on Tuesdays, Thursdays and

Saturdays, and, again, this was a chore the lady of the house usually handled alone. Typically, she produced not only white and brown bread, but also fancy cakes, pastries and pies filled with fruits she had preserved herself.

The importance of cooking and its effects on health were frequently emphasized by lecturers, writers and health reformers. Dr. J. H. Kellogg, founder of the cereal company, stated in 1876, "men and women are subjected to few diseases whose origins may not be traced to the kitchen."[4] Nine years later, another food reformer, Dr. E. G. Cook, said in a magazine article, "There can be no more important subject. The stomach is the centre of life."[5]

North Americans were obsessed with the idea of health. As waves of European immigrants reached the new world, the dominant Anglo-Saxon group became increasingly afraid that they would be overwhelmed by these foreigners with their strange languages and customs, aliens who were almost always stereotyped as dirty, ignorant, and immoral. To add to the Anglo-Saxon paranoia, there was a widespread belief that the race was in a decline, that men, and particularly women, were not as strong or resilient as the illustrious ancestors who had carved a new society out of the North American wilderness. And one of the major factors in this decline was the ill health caused by poor cooking. In an article in a popular magazine, the "American disease", dyspepsia, or chronic indigestion, was discussed. "The prevalence of dyspepsia... is simply the results of a century of bad cookery."[6]

How could a woman learn the cooking skills required to fulfill her domestic duties without endangering her family's health? Most women learned to cook from their mothers, and so continued the tradition responsible for the "century of bad cookery." The more progressive women relied on contemporary magazine articles or the innumerable books on household advice published in the last three decades of the Victorian era.

There were drawbacks to both methods. The books on household advice often provided conflicting information and sometimes the advice was ambiguous or difficult to understand. Relying on cooking skills handed down from generation to generation was not always feasible as technology improved and more and more people moved from rural to urban areas. Additionally, the basics of hygiene and nutrition were only beginning to reach the middle classes, and women who relied on old-fashioned methods of food preparation put their families in danger of food poisoning or worse.

It's possible that the shock of her son, John Harold's death, if it did result from contaminated food, made Adelaide feel guilty about her own ignorance of food handling. Perhaps it was this guilt that turned her into a zealous advocate of food reform. Tenacious, energetic, and insatiably curious about any subject which interested her, she would have read everything she could find on nutrition, hygiene, and cooking, and used her knowledge and considerable powers of persuasion to win others to her cause. So,while she was not a professional cook, she was the guiding spirit behind the YWCA cooking classses.

At least some Hamiltonians were willing to admit the need for cooking classes. Five years earlier, the *Spectator* had printed a letter to the editor:

> I hear so many married ladies complaining on their servants' cooking, and saying they cannot instruct them, as they know very little about it themselves, that I have come to the conclusion that a systematic cooking school is needed in this city at the present time, where old and young, maid and mistress, may learn the principles of good cooking, which may be easily learned by a person of ordinary intelligence in about three months. Good well cooked victuals are necessary to good health. Where there is poor cooking there is inevitably waste and this, added, makes life a burden to the paterfamilias. There are very few natural born cooks, and fewer yet who have both natural and acquired arts of cooking in all dishes common to this country in a first class manner. Will not some one of these "queens of cooking art" open a school in this city, for I am sure from the laments I hear on all sides it would be well patronized. [7]

Adelaide, as one of the "newspaper reading women" of the city, probably read the letter. Obviously, it would have struck a sympathetic chord, and, it may have been one of the factors which inspired her to establish cooking classes.

Adelaide's involvement in the cooking classes left her open to some criticism. She was well known in the Hamilton because of her social connections and work with the YWCA and Local Council. So, for that matter was John. Undoubtedly, some of the criticism levelled at Adelaide resulted from jealousy, either on the part of John's business rivals, or some of Adelaide's colleagues. It is more likely, though, that most of the criticisms which arose were genuine indications of the temper of the times. The underlying theme of these complaints was clear, if illogical: there was no need to teach a woman cookery, since it was something she learned naturally.

Any criticism of Adelaide would inevitably have reflected on John, since, after all, a Victorian husband was completely responsible for his wife's behaviour. Yet there is no hint that he attempted to curtail her activities. In fact, indications are that he did quite the opposite. In a transcript of a speech given shortly before her death, Adelaide credited John with encouraging her to carry out her own work.

> He has been most heartily sympathetic— the fact of the matter is, he made me do lots of things I did not like, in fact he made me go on the public platform when it was most distasteful, but he believed it was my duty. [8]

John Hoodless, was, apparently, a singularly enlightened Victorian husband. It is doubtful that Adelaide, who always needed encouragement and reassurance that her efforts were worthwhile, could have maintained her crusade if John had opposed her involvement.

There are indications that Adelaide was frequently anxious, and definite evidence that she was quick to respond to criticism. Yet criticism was probably the last thing on her mind when she started the YWCA cooking class. She felt well-qualified to advise other women on homemaking. Her various activities outside the home indicate she had reliable household help, who, under her direction, kept the Hoodless home running smoothly. In fact, as her son Bernard would later recall,

> Today one can hardly conceive that the attacks made upon her could have occurred. She was derided in the press and from the platform as one of those despised "new women". "Let her stay home and take care of her family," was one of the pieces of advice most often handed out. As to staying at home and taking care of her family, well! No mother was ever more devoted, nor any home better managed.... She was a great mother, and her wonderfully developed mother's instinct was large enough to include all classes and creeds. I think I could describe her no better than to say she was a woman with a great maternal instinct.[9]

Apparently Adelaide was a superb cook who baked the most delicious cookies, and the children of the neighbourhood often dropped in to share them with Edna, Bernard, and Muriel. There is also a tantalizing hint that, beneath her no-nonsense exterior was a heart bursting with Victorian sentimentality. Among the Hoodless family papers is a note addressed to "Santa Claus, Cleveland, Ohio." Dated December 1893, it was written by nine-year old Edna while she was staying with her aunt in Ohio. In a childish scrawl, Edna politely asks for a fair-haired doll, an alley, and a "box of colors."[10] It's easy to imagine Adelaide's sister-in-law handing her the note with an amused smile, and to see Adelaide storing it away as a souvenir of her elder daughter's childhood.

The ability to care for her family and keep her home running smoothly while she dedicated herself to various causes were but two of Adelaide's many talents. She also possesed considerable charm, and it was this, as much as her wit and intelligence, which made many of those acquainted with her devoted allies.

At first glance, there would seem to have been few pressures in her life which might have soured her charming personality. She was married to a well-to-do businessman, and the Hoodless family enterprise flourished during the early years of their marriage. After his father's retirement, John became manager of the company, and branched out into the "manufacture of artistic interior hardwood for mantels, stairways... partitions, flooring, etc."[11] Under John's guidance, the company installed the interiors of such new buildings as the Sun Life Insurance Company in Hamilton and the Royal College of Dental Surgeons in Toronto.

The Hoodless reputation was a fine one. In 1884, the firm won the only gold medal ever issued to a furniture exhibit up to that time by the Toronto Industrial Exhibition Association. Later, the company won international awards in London and Antwerp. Because of the success of the business, John was able to maintain his household in fine style. Eastcourt, the home they moved into in 1893, was described as

> a magnificent, palatial residence... standing in the midst of four acres and considered one of the handsomest in the city of Hamilton. Its architectural beauty is supplemented by many beautiful works of art and the adornments which wealth can secure and refined taste suggest.[12]

But even the most hard-working and successful people experience setbacks. First, there was the shock of the company going into receivership. Eventually, the company recovered. Then another disaster threatened. Early on the morning of 22 December 1892, a fire broke out at the Ontario Box Company on Main Street near Catharine, right beside the Hoodless factory. A message was sent to John, who hurried to the fire while Adelaide waited anxiously at home. Although firemen trained six hoses on the fire at the box company, neighbouring buildings were in considerable danger. By the time the blaze was extinguished, the box factory was a total loss and the Hoodless factory suffered some damage from flames and water, although a major disaster was averted.

Adelaide took the problem in her stride. She was simply too busy with her various community projects to spend time brooding. Gradually, her memories of Chicago and the inspirational speeches she had heard there, coupled with her own reading and conversations with other women, made it clear to her that something must be done to educate women on household management. The cooking classes at the YWCA were only the first step, a small foothold in what would become a full-fledged national campaign.

By this time, Adelaide had become convinced that the teaching of domestic science was absolutely essential to the quality of Canadian life. She had apprently evolved her opinions gradually after observing the girls who came to the YWCA. Many years later she would describe the process that led to her convicitons:

> I associated with girls chiefly from the commercial class, such as type-writers, office workers, shop girls— the majority of the girls of the YWCA belong to the commercial class — that was where I got my first inspiration in domestic science — I found, after this association with these girls for a great many years, that they were being commercialized; we had typewriters provided in our schools; we were offering everything to enable them to fill commercial occupations, and we were not doing one thing to develop the domestic side. In other words, we were trying to draft [sic] masculine tendencies on feminine stock, and that has been the tendency of our system of education for some years.[13]

Adelaide exaggerated in saying she had associated with these girls "for many years." What is more likely is that she had been impressed by what she had heard or read on domestic science, and, having become convinced that education in the field was necessary, looked around for a means to substantiate her beliefs. In Adelaide's opinion, the school system was at fault, and certainly she could claim familiarity with the system because of John's involvement in the Board of Education. Because schools emphasized a classical education for boys and girls alike, Adelaide felt young women were unprepared for their primary work as wives and mothers. She wanted courses instituted to teach women the basics of nutrition and hygiene, as well as household management.

> Girls should be educated to fit them properly for the sphere of life for which they are destined, that of homemaking, and this should be done by teaching domestic science in the public schools.[14]

Adelaide would say, "Educate a boy and you educate a man, but educate a girl and you educate a family."[15]

The concept of domestic science was fairly new in the United States and Britain, newer still in Canada, so Adelaide frequently was required to define it and explain its importance. she did so with clarity and flair.

> Domestic Science is the application of scientific principles to the management of the home. It teaches the value of pure air, proper food, systematic management, economy, care of children, domestic and civil sanitation and the prevention of disease. It calls for higher and higher ideals of home life and more respect for domestic occupations. In short, it is a direct education for women as homemakers. The management of the home has more to do in the moulding of character than any other influence, owing to the large place it fills in the early life of the individual during the most plastic stage of development. We are, therefore, justified in an effort to secure a place for home economics or domestic science, in the education institutions of this country.[16]

Strange as it seems today, the domestic science movement was partly inspired by nineteenth-century feminists who saw it as a means of elevating woman's work to the level of a profession. In effect, domestic science was an attempt to put housework — woman's work — on a par with man's work. Adelaide may not have been in favour of female suffrage, but she certainly did not believe that women were less capable than men.

Yet Adelaide may also have begun to realize that there could be trouble winning the support of the Local Council of Women in her battle to introduce domestic science education in Hamilton. Already the new organization was beset by internal difficulties, including a power struggle between Adelaide's supporters and those of Local Council president Mary Rose Holden.

At a meeting on 13 March, a motion was made to introduce the minutes of the preceeding meeting. Adelaide promptly objected, ''upon the grounds that, the previous meetings have been held under provisional officers, the minutes could not be passed with provisional officers still acting.''[17]

A heated debate ensued. Mrs. Rose Holden insisted she was elected president for a regular term of office, but other ladies objected, with Adelaide arguing that the Local Council could not have regularly elected officers unless it had formally affiliated with the National Council and paid its dues, which had not been the case when the provisional officers were elected. After more discussion, most of the executive, including Adelaide, who was corresponding secretary, resigned. Mrs. Rose Holden did not.

As nominations for a new slate of officers began, Adelaide refused to allow her name to stand for the position of corresponding secretary. Bertha Savage was elected in her place. Was Adelaide's refusal a matter of principle, an objection to the lack of regard for organizational procedure, especially on Mary Rose Holden's part? Or was it a more personal objection? The Local Council was becoming divided into a Hoodless and anti-Hoodless faction. Although Mrs. Holden's tenacious grasp on the presidency was a point scored against the Hoodless faction, Adelaide attempted to get the last word in— at least on paper:

> Mrs. Hoodless, who did not appear to be entirely in accord with the head of the Local Council, gave an address upon retiring from office, the address affirming her belief in the good to be accomplished by the National Council of Women, and expressing a hope that the Local Council would be guided in the spirit in which the National Council was founded.[18]

The address, which was printed in the *Hamilton Spectator*, also made pointed reference to the events of the meeting:

> You are called upon to-day to perform your first responsible duty — to elect your officers for the year.... You must choose wisely and carefully. Your president should be a woman capable of giving all necessary information with courtesy and dignity; one who will be able to attend a meeting of any federating society, if invited, and give wise counsel, and one who will have the confidence of the Council as their representative.[19]

Was Adelaide implying that Mary Rose Holden lacked these qualities, and that someone else, perhaps Adelaide herself, possessed them? Certainly that was how Mrs. Holden interpreted the events of the meeting. In a front page story in the *Hamilton Times*, she defended her own actions and referred to Adelaide's speech, ''much of which I think was uncalled for... I think that desire for office is the secret of a great deal of the trouble.''[20]

Adelaide declined to make a statement to the *Times* or to have anything further to do with the Local Council under the existing circumstances. She could bide her time.

Chapter Five

A School of Domestic Science

At any rate, Adelaide was not about to let factional disagreements divert her. After she presented her views on domestic science education to the Local Council, she was asked to prepare a resolution for submission to the National Council convention, scheduled for April. Adelaide happily complied, and the *Spectator* reported her remarks on 3 April 1894.

> A common argument in regard to industrial training for girls is that home should be the school for industrial knowledge. How many homes can be taken as types of what a true home should be? And how can a woman teach what she does not know herself, and in many cases not had the opportunity to learn before assuming the management of a home and children...let us look at the present system. The mind is educated while the executive functions have been neglected. The faculties that deal with the realities of life are crowded out of existence by theories and indolent habits are acquired through too constant attention to books.[1]

The force of her personality, the logic of her arguments, and the fact that she was a highly placed member of the National Council combined to win approval of the resolution from the Local Council. Now it was up to Adelaide to convince the National Council of women of the righteousness of her crusade.

The first annual convention of the National Council opened at ten o'clock on 11 April in the convocation hall of the Ottawa Normal school. One hundred and fifty people, including a handful of men, gathered amid flowers and flags to hear Lady Aberdenn's opening remarks. Then Emily Cummings, secretary of the National Council, reported on the formation of local councils across the country and the number of societies which were federated with them. Montreal led the list with thirty-two federated societies, followed by Ottawa with twenty-seven and Hamilton with twenty-five.

A large proportion of the conference was taken up by the reading of papers. Delegates spoke on charity work, the need to organize women workers, child guidance (including a paper by Mrs. Fréchette on "Difficult Children and How to Undertsand Them"), as well as art, music and literature. In the evening, Lord and Lady Aberdeen hosted a reception at Rideau Hall, which was attended by members of parliament and Ottawa society as well as the conference delegates.

On the afternoon of 12 April, Adelaide read her paper. Initially, she seemed cautious, then gradually warmed to her subject.

> The very magnitude of the subject I have dared to introduce for the consideration of the National Council almost overwhelms me when I attempt to give a reason for bringing the question before this influential organization. "Fools rush in where angels fear to tread," may seem applicable in this case; but I am willing to endure criticism and even harsh judgment if I may only succeed in impressing the importance of this question upon the women of Canada.
>
> * * *
>
> Were I to treat the subject simply from a theoretical standpoint I would not, I fear, accomplish my purpose. What I hope to do is, to arouse an interest in the question and then you will learn for yourselves what eminent educational authorities have to say concerning it, in the many publications to be found in our public libraries, book stores, etc.[2]

Adelaide then referred to the works of various writers and spoke on the progress which had been made in England and the United States in the field of domestic science. She pointed out the benefits of such studies in preventing divorces, "if practical knowledge formed part of the education of every girl we would not see so many domestic shipwrecks,"[3] and reducing waste, "A reliable statistician says... that bad management and ignorance in cooking wastes $500,000,000 of food every year in the United States."[4] Then she urged local councils to work towards the establishment of domestic science programs in their schools.

To further intrigue her audience, Adelaide explained how the programmes could be set up.

> The first step will be to introduce the kitchengarden, or as Miss Huntington, the founder of the system says, it should have been called the domestic kindergarten.... Small tables are set with all the necessary dishes, cutlery, napkins, etc., and real dinners are served and eaten by little ones. Beds are made properly, paper folding gives place to stocking darning and knitting....[5]

In the higher grades, she emphasized the need for alternating demonstrations with practice, "so that the faculty of imitation, generally large in children, may be called into useful exercise."[6] She pointed to programmes in effect in Germany, and concluded with a resolution:

> That the National Council of Women do all in its power to further the introduction of industrial (or manual) training for girls in the public school system of Canada, believing that such training will greatly conduce to the general welfare of Canadian homes, and that copies of this resolution be sent to the ministers of education of each provincial government.[7]

The resolution was passed, an outcome influenced not only by Adelaide's paper but by comments from such prestigious women as Dr. Emily Howard Stowe. Dr. Stowe remarked on the abyssmal conditions she often encountered while making her rounds, conditions that could be directly traced to the lack of training in domestic science. And Lady Aberdeen added her support to Adelaide's arguments when she said, "We believe implicitly that the home is the woman's first mission."[8] As a result, a standing committee on Domestic Science and Technical Training was organized, with Adelaide as national convenor. Subsequently she became convenor of the committee in Hamilton as well.

In winning the support of the National Council on the subject of domestic science, Adelaide created a powerful network which would help prepare the way for its introduction in the school systems of Canada. At the very least, the women would discuss the events of the convention with friends and colleagues on their return home. At best, they would begin to make demands for programmes in their own areas, where women like Adelaide were already breaking ground in domestic science education. In either case, they helped further the cause of domestic science, a cause which would bring Adelaide considerable public recognition.

But first, there was the problem with the Hamilton Local Council. On Saturday, 19 May, members of Hamilton's Local Council gathered for a meeting. They were supposed to read the papers delegates had presented to the National Council convention, however a crisis in the organization delayed the readings.

Because the meeting had been hastily called, only 25 women gathered in the Board of Trade rooms. Notably absent was Local Council president, Mary Rose Holden. Mrs. George Papps presided in her place, and her first item of business was to read Mary Holden's letter of resignation. The letter was brief, and the reason for it was soon made clear. Mrs. Holden had signed a memo on prison reform on behalf of the Local Council and instructed Bertha Savage, the corresponding secretary to mail it. However, as Mrs. Papps "indignantly"[9] pointed out, few of the Local Council members had heard the details of the issue, which had only-90-Feen discussed in Ottawa.

The fact that Bertha Savage was not asked to resign indicates she probably informed Adelaide and the Local Council executive of Mrs. Holden's unilateral action. Although the *Times* reporter refrained from mentioning any comments made by the membership regarding Mrs. Holden's presumptuousness, it was apparent that the women of the Local Council — at least those who attended the meeting— were tired of Mrs. Holden's highandedness. Adelaide was probably expressing the sentiments of the majority when she complained, "Mrs. Holden has had the entire management of the affairs of the Council.... We are not a bit further advanced as a society than we were November last."[10]

Needless to say, Mary Rose Holden's resignation was accepted by a unanimous vote. For Adelaide, it was a triumphant finale in her battle with Mrs. Holden for power within the Local Council. Now that her friends were in control of the executive, Adelaide could easily persuade the Local Council to support her interests.

Having got the unpleasantness of Mary Holden's resignation out of the way, the ladies ended the meeting on a lighter note. Adelaide reported on the Ottawa convention, ending with an amusing story about Senator Sanford. At the convention, both Wilfrid Laurier and John Thompson had become patrons of the Council. Sanford expressed a wish to add his name to the list, but was called away on business before arrangements were finalized. Mrs. Papps telegrammed him to ask him whether he wished to be a Local Council patron or a National Council patron. Apparently, the senator was not aware that a donation of $100 was required to become a National Council patron, compared to $50 for the local organization. He wired back that the decision was in Mrs. Papp's hands, and she promptly made him a patron of the national society.

"'And, of course, the National Society needs the money,'' remarked Mrs. Hoodless with a rich tinge of humour."[11]

Adelaide's sense of humour was to be frequently strained in the cause of domestic science. Soon after their return from Ottawa, a deputation of ladies from the Local Council called on the Hamilton Board of Education. Adelaide read a paper she had prepared with Mrs. Papps, which began by reiterating the National Council's approval of the introduction of domestic science classes in public schools. She explained that the women had no intention of lowering the standards of the school curriculum by removing necessary subjects in order to make room for domestic science. Nevertheless, they considered domestic science of paramount importance.

> Upon the education of the Canadian school girl depends the future of the Canadian home. The science of home life should keep pace with improvements in outside affairs. Why should a daughter go on making bad bread and the indigestible mixtures her mother and grandmother inflicted upon their families?[12]

After citing similar programmes in other countries and quoting experts, including a teacher of "sanitary chemistry" at the Massachusetts Institute of Technology, the ladies requested three things:

> 1. That classes in cooking and sewing be added to the curriculum of the Hamilton public schools; that girls in three higher grades be given two lessons a week in cooking and two lessons in sewing; that the five grades receive instruction in sewing in two lessons a week of half an hour or an hour as may be most expedient, and that competent teachers be provided for each department.

> 2. That this committee begs that accomodation be provided for these classes in the two new schools to be erected.

3. This committee begs to recommend that the experiment be tried in one school this year.[13]

In an attempt to persuade the Board, Mrs. Papps indicated there was already public support for the project: "a number of friends have promised medals for the competition."[14] Furthermore, the Hamilton Gas Company had offered to supply a gas range and fuel for an experimental kitchen. To add further weight to the argument, Mrs. Lyle said that Minister of Education George Ross seemed in favour of the project.

The reaction of the Board can only be described as cautiously favourable. One trustee, J. J. Mason, suggested the ladies should first receive Ministry approval. He also pointed out that the project, while worthwhile, would be expensive, and the Board had recently come under fire for the introduction of kindergarten classes. Moreover, there was a question of legality. The Ministry had not, as far as he was aware, granted permission to boards to hire teachers of domestic science. Consequently, "he could not see that the board could hold out much hope to the ladies— at least for some time to come."[15] However, Mason added there would be no harm in referring the matter to the International Management Committee, and a resolution to that effect was passed.

Despite the polite reception, no progress was made in starting domestic science classes in Hamilton schools. But Adelaide was not about to ignore any avenues which might lead to her goal. She and the ladies who had called on the Board of Education made the trip to Toronto and spoke with George Ross.

At the suggestion of the Honourable J. M. Gibson, whose wife was a member of the delegation, the women first presented a short argument detailing the advantages of domestic and manual training for boys and girls. Then they presented their resolution:

> That the Minister of Education of the Province of Ontario be requested to ammend the public school law regulations so as to provide 1st that the Board of Education, high school, public school and separate school trustees in any city, town or municipality may by resolution passed at a regular meeting of the board adopt a course of manual training, comprising the study and practice of domestic science, and such branches as may be deemed suitable for boys, subject to the approval of the board of education.[16]

The women further requested that similar courses be offered to high school students.

While Ross was polite, he could offer no encouragement. But Adelaide was not willing to give up easily. Did she appeal to his pride, arguing that Ontario should not fall behind other areas in its educational system? A one-time teacher and journalist, Ross was both ambitious and reform-minded. He had already fought for the introduction of music and physical education in Ontario schools. So, when Adelaide urged him to visit American schools

George W. Ross, Minister of Education, later Premier of Ontario. A former teacher, Ross became an avid supporter of Adelaide's domestic science crusade: his daughter graduated from a domestic science course.

where domestic science was taught, he wavered. By the end of the meeting, Adelaide had extracted a promise from Ross to visit the Pratt and Cooper Institutes in New York and the technical schools in Boston.

True to his word, Ross did visit the schools. While he continued to oppose manual training for boys, he was sufficiently impressed with what he saw to ask Adelaide to draft an amendment to the Education Act which would allow domestic science education in public schools. Adelaide happily undertook the assignment, although she was burdened with personal problems.

That summer had been difficult for Adelaide. John's mother died in August, and his father moved to Eastcourt. By this time Joseph Hoodless had been retired for a decade and was suffering from heart trouble, complicated by dropsy. The additional burden of caring for her ailing and bereft father-in-law must have been a trial to Adelaide, but, in her usual fashion, she managed as best she could without neglecting the duties that had become so close to her heart.

The amendment was drafted and sent to the Toronto Local Council for approval. It was rapidly rejected as half-hearted, since it excluded manual training for boys. The Toronto Local Council sent a revised amendment back to Hamilton, promising their support if manual training was included. Another delegation visited the Minister of Education, and somehow George Ross was persuaded to agree to the new approach. He suggested that a "memorial" be sent to the government, requesting a change in legislation.

Meanwhile, plans were being finalized for a school of domestic science to be run under the auspices of the Hamilton YWCA. The reasoning behind this move was simple: if the school board would not provide facilities for the teaching of domestic science, the YWCA would do its best to fill the gap. The *Spectator* of 22 September dwelt at great length on the topics to be covered in the domestic science course, including sewing:

> On Tuesday afternoon next the annual meeting of the Young Women's Christian Association will be held in the parlours of the building no. 17 Main Street West. Interesting addresses will be given. A new branch of the work has been inaugurated — the School of Domestic Science, which, it is hoped, may prove a benefit to the public. Classes have been arranged in cooking, sewing, home dressmaking, and millinery. There will be both morning and evening classes. The course in educational sewing includes a drill in all stitches used in making fine underwear, infants clothing and plain dressmaking. The housekeeper's course includes plain sewing, darning, mending rents and table linen, grafting for underwear, etc. In the dressmaking measures are taken and patterns drafted by the tailor square system. Making dresses in a plain manner and millinery will also be taught. The course in cookery is most thorough and practical, aiming to teach economical, yet attractive cookery, advanced and fancy work not being omitted. Many young women of

refinement, culture and intelligence have a very superficial knowledge of many things. The aim of the Hamilton School of Domestic Science is to make women real homemakers.[17]

The importance of sewing for women of 1894 cannot be underestimated. Although ready-made garments were increasingly available, sewing still remained one of the most onerous, time-consuming tasks required of middle class women. Not only were wives and mothers expected to keep the linen, towels and pillowcases in good repair, they were also expected to sew the bulk of the family's wardrobe, everything from men's shirts, cuffs, and collars to their own fashionable dresses. They were expected to knit socks, scarves, and other woolen garments for the winter months, too, and whenever an article of clothing became worn or went out of fashion, they were expected to remake it into something more suitable.

While commercial patterns were available, these were much more complicated than those of today, partly because of the styles of clothing, but also because the seamstress generally had to trace the pattern pieces onto separate sheets of paper in order to use them. Unless a woman was fortunate enough to own a sewing machine, one of the most blessed time-saving devices of the era, or could borrow one from a friend, she did all the sewing by hand. The time she spent in sewing was staggering by modern standards: a man's shirt could take fourteen and a half hours to complete! While public opinion, as evidenced by comments in *Godey's Magazine*, deplored too much sewing as ''nothing but a dull round of everlasting toil, and too often have eyesight and health, as well as hopes and spirits, sunk under the burden,''[18] at the same time women were expected to be highly adept with needle and thread. To be unable to sew one's own clothing was a terrible disgrace. And, should a woman's economic position free her from the necessity of making her family's wardrobe, she was still expected to ply the needle, by making decorative objects for the home or gifts for loved ones. Idleness was a sin in the minds of the Victorian middle class. A man was expected to work hard, to make his business flourish, while his wife ran the home. If wealth allowed the hiring of a domestic servant, the wife should still busy herself with various needlework projects and fancy cooking as proof of her homemaking skills.

The YWCA meeting held on 26 September marked the beginning of the fifth year for the Hamilton organization. Before the meeting, and during interludes in business, Mrs. Fenwick sang, accompanied by Professor Aldous on the piano. Several annual reports were given, including one by General Secretary Anna C. Helm, who discussed some of the prejudices the YWCA had encountered.

> Our work is not... in any sense a reformative work, but rather an educational and spiritual one. No little blame is attached to us because we are not doing the rescue in connection with our legitimate work, but a little thoughtful consideration will show the impossibility of combining the

two. People have said to us, "I thought you professed to be governed by the spirit of Christ. Is it Christ like to turn your back upon those other young women who have made a shipwreck of virtue, and refuse them a helping hand back to life again?" No, not Christ like, perhaps, and we wish it were far otherwise, but so long as social custom and demands remain as they are, experience has taught us that such work must always be distinctive and special, and must come within the scope of mission and rescue work.[19]

Sex was never far from Victorian minds, as Helm's comments demonstrate, although what was publicly discussed was much more likely to be the evils rather than the joys of it. Hand-in-hand with the notion that women were frail creatures who must be protected from contaminating influences went the idea of the "fallen woman." Loss of virginity outside the marriage bed meant utter ruin for a Victorian girl, particularly if she became pregnant. She could realistically expect to be abandoned by family and friends under such circumstances; she was also very likely to lose her job. Cut off from emotional and financial support, such women had little choice but to turn to prostitution and crime.

Consequently, many charitable organizations existed to help these desperate women, and, as Anna Helm pointed out, it was assumed that any women's organization would automatically be engaged in rescue work. The YWCA was not, hence the criticism. Yet, as Miss Helm said, it was really a matter of common sense, Victorian style. While Victorians might praise attempts to rehabilitate women of dubious virtue, such women could not come into regular social contact with society's morally upright maids and matrons. To have a fallen woman sleep under the same roof and share the same parlour as a virtuous working girl was unthinkable, particularly if the working girl was far from home and family influences. So the YWCA did not engage in "the rescue", yet it may have prevented many young women from falling into evil by offering spiritual guidance, shelter, and, above all, classes which could help them obtain employment, or, at the very least, keep them constructively occupied.

Thus, despite the critics the Hamilton YWCA could be proud of its record as it entered its fifth year of activity. In addition to running physical education classes under the Misses Bowditch, Henderson and Smith, the organization offered voice culture, French and bookkeeping courses, and had opened a second branch at the old Customs House on Stuart Street. The establishment of domestic science classes was, to some extent, an extension of the YWCA's committment to practical education for women.

Naturally, there were grumblings in the city, echoing the comments that were made when cooking classes were introduced. Surely this information could be obtained at home, the critics argued. Adelaide and her supporters ignored them, dwelling instead on the praise they received for their efforts.

One parent wrote of his feelings on the subject in a letter to the editor of the *Spectator*:

> With others, I was, through a strong belief in the benefits of practical education, impelled to pay a call at the school of Domestic Science, which name is new to our ears, and which implies so much that goes toward the well-being and comfort of mankind. It was a revelation, and the Young Women's Christian Association and its energetic officers deserve the warmest thanks of the citizens generally for being the first, I believe, in Canada, to boldly start such a school. Well do they deserve encouragement, and as a father I am thankful that my daughters will have an opportunity of broadening an education that will be of a lasting practical benefit to them and the homes they may preside over in the future at a cost that is within the reach of nearly all. The kitchen is simply perfect, with its three square tables for four pupils at each table, the accomplished instructresses in uniform similar to the students; the gas stove and small heaters, the pretty china dinner set and the bright pleasant room, not only elevates the work of the kitchen in every sense, but puts it on the level of a science. Those who have never imagined what can be done to improve the everyday food we eat, and to obtain the very best results, both as regards value and nutrition, should at once seriously consider the taking of a course at this school. Manual training is going to be a course that will receive special attention in our public schools, as anyone can see who is visiting the advanced centres or studying the trend of education. This school will provide an opportunity for Hamilton to keep in advance and have competent teachers of sewing and cookery, when they will be required.[20]

Adelaide could hardly have said it better herself.

Chapter Six

A Controversial Crusade

Over the next two years, Adelaide would make a concerted effort to turn the resolutions of the Local and National Councils into reality. She was helped by the fact that she held high profile posts in both the National Council and the YWCA. On 23 January 1895, she was elected president of the Dominion YWCA *in absentia*. Although she had been unable to attend the convention, her papers on the influence of the organization and the education work it was undertaking were read by her friend, Mrs. Charlton.

Her election must have been a topic of interest when the Hamilton YWCA held its annual meeting on 26 February. Adelaide must have been particularly pleased at the recognition accorded her, and perhaps a little smug as well. Both she and John were becoming increasingly prominent in Hamilton's social and business world: only a few days earlier, John had been elected president of the newly-formed Canadian Retail Furniture Dealers Association.

There were more triumphs to come, but first it was necesssary to increase support for the Local and National Councils of Women. On 5 March, Lady Aberdeen arrived in Hamilton to publicize the work of the Council. The occasion almost turned into a disaster. To begin with there was a problem with travel because of a recent snowstorm. Originally, Lady Aberdeen was scheduled to speak at a 1:30 luncheon, but, because of the snow, the women turned the luncheon into a 4:30 dinner. According to Lady Aberdeen, ''the train being late again made it a 5:30 affair, & all the eatables somewhat chilly, & the ladies decidedly self-conscious that something out of the way was going on.''[1]

The eatables included chicken consomme followed by fish, beef, and turkey entrées. There was a wide selection of desserts to complete the meal, including orange jelly, charlotte russe, strawberry tartlets, vanilla ice cream, malaga grapes, pineapples, oranges, almonds, raisons, and apples, followed by tea and coffee. Notably absent was wine: because many of the female activists were also staunch temperence advocates, it was considered unseemly to serve alcoholic beverages. How much attention was paid to the dinner itself is disputable, since the event at the Royal Hotel was something of a novelty. There were no men present, a fact which the Hamilton newspapers remarked on. One curious consequence of the absence of both men and liquor was the spectacle of the upstanding women of Hamilton proposing toasts— which were drunk in water.

Following the meal, the dinner guests moved to the opera house, where a large group of women had gathered to hear Lady Aberdeen. Several male dignitaries joined them, too, among them Senator Sanford, Adam Brown, Mayor Stewart, and Judge Muir. A handful of women sat with them on the platform as Lady Aberdeen addressed the gathering.

"They begged me to go over the old story of the Council again," Lady Aberdeen wrote in her diary, "and so it was the old story, with only a little excursion outside about manual training."[2] By this time, she must have been increasingly bored with having to repeat the story of the Council's founding and stressing the fact that it was not a suffrage organization. Perhaps the "excursion" into manual training was a welcome change. Certainly Lady Aberdeen voiced her wholehearted support of the movement, publicly complimenting Adelaide for her efforts in the field. There was a second, more subtle compliment to Adelaide as well. As a token of appreciation, Lady Aberdeen was presented with flowers by two young girls, Marguerite Papps and twelve-year old Edna Hoodless.

A little more than a month later, Adelaide and her supporters called on George Ross once again. At this time, apparently, he claimed he had no idea how domestic science could be implemented in the schools without great difficulty. However, he did offer to support the ladies in their effort to persuade the Hamilton Board of Education to introduce domestic science.

Around this time, possibly as a result of the meeting with Ross, the Hamilton Board of Education established a committee to look into the question of manual training and domestic science in Hamilton. While awaiting the outcome of the investigation, Adelaide attended the National Council of Women conference in Toronto.

To celebrate the opening of the conference, Lord and Lady Aberdeen held an "at home" in the Toronto legislative chambers. Seated on two easy chairs on a flower-decked dais, the vice-regal couple greeted guests for two hours. Adelaide was among them, wearing a black silk dress trimmed with jet, and a corsage of white roses. So were Madame Laurier, Mrs. Clifford Sifton, and Lady Gzowski. This was probably one of the most prestigious social events Adelaide had yet attended, and her reaction to it can only be guessed. Did she stop to reflect how far she had travelled from her modest St. George farm house? If she did, she had little time to dwell on the fact, for the first Council meeting got under way at ten o'clock the following morning.

Adelaide naturally took every opportunity to advance her pet cause. (She sometimes went to extremes— that same year, when asked to officiate at the opening of a new fruit market in Hamilton, she made a point of declaring how much a new fruit market would benefit domestic science students!) Whether she made any new converts at the Council meetings is unknown, and not particularly relevant. While Adelaide probably envisaged domestic science in schools from coast to coast, in 1895 she was primarily concerned with domestic science at the local level.

Two weeks after the Council conference, the committee to investigate manual training and domestic science reported to the Hamilton Board of Education. Although the school inspector Ballard had provided testimonials on the benefits of manual training from schools in Woodstock, Montreal, and Halifax, committee chairman Alex Turner vetoed similar programmes in Hamilton. The problem, as before, was money. However, he offered some consolation. Because it was felt that sewing could easily be taught by regular grade school teachers, it was suggested that this could be added to the curriculum without undue disruption of existing programmes.

It was a step in the right direction, but not a large enough step for Adelaide. Shortly after the committee made its recommendations, the YWCA sent another letter to the Board of Education, again requesting the introduction of domestic science. While the matter was under consideration, the Hoodless family was struggling with another loss. Joseph Hoodless succumbed to old age and illness on July 4th, less than a year after his wife's demise. During the last months of his life, the old man had been bedridden, and if Adelaide and John mourned his death, they must also have welcomed the end to his suffering.

There was financial compensation for their loss as well. Joseph Hoodless left an estate of $75,000, a small fortune by the standards of 1895, to be divided among John and his two sisters. John inherited Eastcourt (valued at $7,500), his father's interest in the furniture company, and a warehouse on Catharine Street. He also received a considerable amount of cash, part of which was used to pay off the $6,000 mortgage on the house.

There was little time to dwell on this latest loss, or the financial benefit it brought, however. In addition to teaching cooking classes, Adelaide was busy defending domestic science at every turn. In the *Hamilton Evening Times* of 21 September 1895, she wrote:

> In reply to your query expressed in the Times last evening concerning the time necessary for teaching sewing and cooking in the Public Schools.... In the first place I quite agree with you in bewailing the too numerous studies already inflicted upon the children, especially in the Collegiate and would be most reluctant to add one iota of additional work to either teacher or pupil.... We do not propose introducing these subjects into the Collegiate Institute, at least not at present; the time may come when they will desire it. Sewing begins in kindergarten and is carried through various grades until the two higher ones are reached, when it stops and cooking takes its place.... While one hour a week is sufficient for sewing, two hours are required for a lesson in domestic science as this includes... practical chemistry, hygiene, sanitation, care of food.... I venture to say that nine-tenths of the sensible parents in this city would appreciate the practical benefits resulting from a thorough training in sewing and cooking more than a brilliant discourse on the number of rivers in Africa... domestic science is...not simply teaching children how to cook... but thorough training in domestic economy. What has been satisfactorily arranged in other places can be in Hamilton.[3]

But it would not be arranged in Hamilton in the immediate future, at least not in the public school system. However, there were some small steps forward before the year's end. At a YWCA meeting in late September, Bertha Wright of Ottawa, addressed the topic of domestic science, and showed "views" — photographic slides— of the activities at the YWCA school. When pictures of the instructor, Miss Wilson, and Adelaide, were shown, the audience applauded enthusiastically. And, as if that were not enough to bolster Adelaide's spirits, Miss Wright also complimented the Hamilton YWCA for establishing the first such school in Canada.

Nor was the support of Adelaide's crusade limited to women's organizations. On 20 October, a letter from the Hamilton Trades and Labour Council was read to the Board of Education. In it, the Council approved the introduction of domestic science as part of the school curriculum, thus adding another, decidedly masculine voice to the cry for domestic science.

In later years, Adelaide would take credit for that particular coup. "I unhesitatingly say where the trades and labor people thoroughly understand the question there will not be an objection raised."[4] She recounted how, initially, members of the Trade and Labour Council had objected to manual training in particular, claiming it would result in lost jobs. Adelaide's solution, characteristically, was to use her feminine wiles. She invited a few members of the Council to Eastcourt, and, in her role of charming hostess, convinced them of the merits of industrial training. "They subsequently addressed the labor council in favor of manual training."[5] What she does not mention is how John's prominence in the business world must have helped, especially since, by March 1896, he was president of the Board of Trade.

A further small success came about as the result of a business trip taken by members of the Board of Education. Late in the year, they visited Buffalo and Pittsbugh to examine new heating systems used in schools there. While in Pittsburgh, they also found time to inspect schools of manual training, and, possibly, these visits added more weight to Adelaide's argument in favour of domestic science. Still, no steps were taken in official circles to introduce domestic science as part of the school curriculum. So Adelaide stepped up the campaign.

Throughout 1896, she continued her efforts to introduce domestic science on a municipal, provincial, and national level. In February, the Hamilton Local Council wrote to the Board of Education asking for the introduction of domestic science in public schools. On 12 March, a special committee was formed to consider the move. While the committee was carrying out its investigation, Adelaide and Mrs. Charlton again visited Geroge Ross. The day after the visit, the *Spectator* reported that Adelaide could not be reached, but Mrs. Charlton "...seemed very well satisfied with the result of the Toronto visit."[6] Although she would not elaborate, she hinted that the legislature was about to introduce measures which

Parlour at Eastcourt.

would advance the cause. The article closed with a speculative observation, "The suspicion is that Hamilton will be the headquarters of a recognized teachers' institution of domestic science, perhaps with government aid."[7]

On 14 May, the special committee presented its report to the Internal Management Committee of the Board of Education. While the special committee noted that they had "witnessed with pleasure the work the Council of Women are doing to interest the public in behalf of a wider course of instruction for children,"[8] they remained reluctant to sanction the expenditure required for the introduction of the new subject. However, they noted the women "have fair prospect"[9] of receiving government support for the training of domestic science teachers. When this object is attained, they will have the means not only of training teachers in these departments, but will be in a better position to educate public sentiments in this direction.[10]

The committee opted to wait "until there is a more general expression of public sentiment in favor of such an expenditure."[11]

Adelaide was determined that the public would express such sentiments, not only in Hamilton, but across the country. That same month, the National Council of Women met in Montreal's YWCA building. As usual, Adelaide made a plea for domestic science education, but this time she also spoke of the need for competent teachers and facilities to train them. Noting the dearth of Canadian philanthropists who might be willing to finance such a scheme, she said the government would have to finance a normal school for domestic science teachers. Apparently, despite the difficulties still to be faced, Adelaide had every reason to expect success. She told the National Council

> We have made a very strong effort in Hamilton to secure a Normal School of Domestic Science and Arts in order to affiliate with the Ontario School of Pedagogy. We have every reason to believe that our request will be granted and that a liberal grant will be given by the Ontario Legislature for the purpose.[12]

She estimated that it would cost between thirty and forty thousand dollars to establish the school, and optimistically believed the bulk of the money would be donated by the citizens of Hamilton.

She was, perhaps, justified in her belief, convinced that the idea of a domestic science teacher's college could appeal to all levels of society, especially those concerned with improving the living conditions of the poor. It was precisely this possibility which appealed to the author of a *Spectator* editorial in favour of the school. One of the advantages, the editorial pointed out, was that it would limit the loss of food value "through ill advised expenditure and poor preparation."[13]

The newspaper editorial was just one more indication of growing public support for domestic science and manual training. At the closing exercises of the YWCA school, Adelaide proudly reported enrollment in the regular classes had climbed to 170, fifty more than in 1895. Furthermore, some older students taught sixty girls at Saturday afternoon classes. There were also special ladies classes, assumedly for homemakers wishing to upgrade their skills, in Dundas, with 26 attending. In all, the YWCA school had reached 256 women and girls in 1896, and the calibre of instruction was excellent. As Adelaide pointed out, no official testing procedure existed in Canada, so examination papers were sent to Boston. The results proved that Hamilton students could compete on an equal basis with those in well established centres of domestic science education.

Adelaide had another opportunity to express her views on domestic science in September, when the YWCA biennial convention was held in Hamilton. Lady Aberdeen presided, reason enough for large crowds to turn up at various events. As usual, there were speeches and papers, and, as always, Adelaide urged the need for domestic science education. Recreational activities included a ride on a new radial railway to the beach, as well as a free trolley tour of the city.

In announcing the events of one day of the convention, a Hamilton newspaper reported, ''It is specially desired that the attendance should not be confined to working girls, for others will be welcomed as well.''[14] Although the newspaper did not dwell on it at the time, there were serious problems besetting the YWCA and other women's organizations.

The women's movement which gathered momentum in the late nineteenth century had various goals, the most important of which could be described as the improvement of conditions for women and their families. Much of the impetus for these reforms came as the result of horror at conditions which prevailed in the slums of industrialized countries, conditions publicized by writers such as Charles Dickens. At the same time, religious fervour was growing, and, when combined with a desire for social reform, it became a force to be reckoned with. Organizations sprang up to care for the spiritual welfare of the poor, to dispel the evils of drink, to redress various wrongs done to women and children, and through them, to society. But these organizations were largely composed of well-intentioned women from the upper levels of society. This is hardly surprising: reform work required large doses of time and money, something middle and upper class women possessed in abundance. Working class women, who were the most desperately in need of various reforms, simply did not have the time or money to invest in long term crusades. They were too busy struggling to survive.

The women who ran the organizations, who determined policies, who undertook the work of educating and reforming less fortunate women, were often considered radical in their time. By our standards, perhaps a handful were, but the majority tended to support the status quo, especially in their own milieu. Again, this was hardly surprising. The women who were the moving force behind reforms had been raised in genteel surroundings, or had acquired genteel airs as a result of fortunate marriages. Few had worked except, perhaps, in the professions which were gradually being recognized as suitable for women, most of which were extensions of the typical female duties of caring for the sick, tending the home, educating the young. Few of their daughters would work, except in these professions. For most, the home and family were still the focus of civilzation, hence they adopted a policy of what has been called 'maternal feminism', the extension of 'mothering' roles, such as housekeeping, childcare, health care, and teaching, into public and professional life.

In the typical Victorian home, the husband was the head, although he could be swayed by the most loving influence of a devoted and competent wife. Most Victorian feminists saw their organizations as fulfilling a wifely role, softening the male harshness of government or industry. Few of them were about to break out of that wifely role, and, indeed, had they done so they might have neutralized what good the feminist movement was accomplishing. Men still made the laws in Canada, and few men were so progressive as to wish to be influenced by repellent "new" women. They could, however, accept new ideas, particularly if they were delivered by attractive, feminine women who dressed nicely, possessed all the social graces, including the art of conversation and mild flirtation, and who readily deferred to the superior sex. It would not have been possible for the average working woman to wield influence in this manner, even if they had been able to meet the policy-makers in a social setting. Consequently, the nineteenth-century feminist movement was dominated by a rather conservative, elitist element which tried to bring about reform by working within the constraints of the society in which they lived.

Because of this, many women reformers, including Adelaide, have been accused in retrospect of limited vision, of not going far enough fast enough. Perhaps the most serious criticism levelled at Adelaide has been that she wished to perpetuate here own social class, that one of her reasons for advocating domestic science education was that it would improve the quality of household servants. Certainly, these were expected results of domestic science education, but it is unlikely that they were the only results which concerned Adelaide, if they concerned her at all. Unless she was a complete hypocrite — and there is little evidence to suggest hypocrisy was one of her faults — she honestly believed that domestic science education was the key to social reform. Having convinced herself of this, she held onto the beliefs with all the legendary tenacity of her Irish and Scottish forebears. It was no accident that she referred to her campaign to introduce domestic science as "missionary work."[15] For Adelaide, the campaign had become an almost religious crusade.

By this time, the Department of Education had made public its intentions regarding domestic science courses, just as Mrs. Charlton had predicted. By the end of January 1897, the Ministry of Ontario had set out guidelines for minimum standards of domestic science education in schools wishing to introduce the subject. The Department had also established examination standards for those who wished to become teachers of domestic science. It seemed likely that this move would lessen resistance to its introduction in the provincial schools, and, as a consequence, opponents of the scheme became more vociferous. On 22 September, a critical article appeared in the *London Free Press*, which claimed that domestic science and manual training education were "a glittering fad,"[16] and that, among other things, manual training would flood the market with a surplus of skilled labour.

Somehow, the article came to Adelaide's attention. On 1 October, she wrote a scathing denunciation of the accusations. After pointing out that some members of both labour organizations and the Conservative Party (Ross was a Liberal) supported the proposed legislation, she ridiculed the *Free Press* reporter's claim. "...as the country is already flooded with incompetent editors",[17] she wrote, should English be removed from public schools? She cited examples of successful training programmes in Europe and the United States, and denounced the heavy emphasis on book learning in Canadian schools.

Adelaide also took pains to point out an important facet of manual training:

> The great mistake being made by those who do not understand the question, is in looking at it purely from a utilitarian standpoint, while the object is entirely educational, in the truest sense, and its adoption is never advocated by well informed educationalists on utilitarian grounds.[18]

The educational value was a fundamental component of Adelaide's concept of manual training. She realized, undoubtedly, that domestic science training would make girls competent cooks and seamstresses and house-keepers. This was obvious to most people who favoured domestic science education. What was frequently overlooked, as she pointed out in her letter, was the fact that domestic science education went beyond that. Ideally, it fostered practicality, common sense, as well as the more important aspects of a so-called classical education. For example, working with recipes or doing household accounts taught mathematical skills without the tedium inherent in repetitive school exercises. In Adelaide's opinion, domestic science was not for the unintelligent. Rather, it was for those whose aptitudes did not lie in the direction of book learning. Domestic science and manual training were never meant as second rate substitutes for a scholarly education. Instead, these practical courses of training were supposed to be equally valuable, but decidedly different forms of education. Unfortunately, it was a concept destined to be misunderstood.

Adelaide's swift and furious response to criticism was typical. Domestic science was her baby, and she protected it with the fiercest of maternal instincts, never ignoring an insult or losing an opportunity to further its interests. Now, with provincial backing virtually assured, the campaign to introduce domestic science in Hamilton schools intensified.

Chapter Seven

The Campaign Heats Up

In the second week of October, the Hamilton Board of Education's Internal Management Committee was again faced with a request from the YWCA. This time, the ladies were asking for two things, the appointment of competent instructors, and the use of an abandoned building on Hunter Street. As ususal, the request was turned down, this time after a lengthy debate in which Chairman Mason insisted there was no public demand for domestic science education. According to the *Spectator*, the formal request to the Board of Education was also accompanied by a letter to Clerk Beasley. In it,

> Mrs. Hoodless intimated that the domestic science committee did not intend to drop the question, and if its members cannot do anything else they can make the trustees study the question.[1]

Such tactics were not guaranteed to win support, particularly when the Board of Education was worried about criticism from other quarters. The estimated cost of $1,000 required to run domestic science classes in the school was a price they considered much too high.

There may have been a second reason for the refusal, too, exemplified by a letter which had been read to the Board of Education. Signed John H. Gordon, it was harshly critical of the proposed domestic science class.

> We have had some experience of teachers of cooking (imported by the Y.W.C.A.) whose colossal ignorance made them the laughing stock of butchers and even of ordinary cooks; but I presume the National Council desired to provide (at the city's expense) a place with a large salary for the graduates of Her Excellency's cooking schools, though which of those so generous ladies would pay a sum to her domestics, who work all day from daylight to dark, Sunday included, is open to discussion.... Our taxes are heavy enough without adding to their burdens merely to gratify the desire for public notoriety that exists in Mrs. Hoodless and others of her stamp, whose love for humanity is shown in their treatment of their dependents.[2]

Ironically, the personal attack on Adelaide inspired a demonstration of public support. "A Citizen" wrote to the paper lauding Adelaide and domestic science, as well as suggesting "John H. Gordon" was a fictitious name. Citizen expressed horror that the school trustees had allowed the letter to be read

> not for the purpose of discussing the question of domestic science in the schools, but of using the board as a medium for a malicious and uncalled

for attack upon a most estimable lady.... Of course the writer of the anonymous letter has gained his end, which was that of striking a coward's blow at a woman. It is a pity the school trustees assisted him to do so.[3]

The *Hamilton Spectator* took the matter a step further, stating that the letter

> would be unworthy of notice but for its spiteful reference to a Hamilton lady who is among the most active, able and disinterested of those engaged in philanthropic and educational work in this city. The writer of that letter penned a mean and cruel libel of Mrs. Hoodless.[4]

The *Herald* described how Adelaide, rather than seeking publicity, had protested over the publication of her name in connection with her various activities. Then the article hypothesized as to the identity of the author of the letter. Pointing out that there was no John H. Gordon in the city directory, the *Herald* surmised,

> It is more likely that a woman wrote that letter. It is just such an epistle as would be conceived and despatched by a spiteful and jealous female, one who is subject to the weaknesses which she attributes to Mrs. Hoodless, one who is perhaps a "friend" of Mrs. Hoodless and greets her in public and private with a sweet smile. There are such feline females with the velvety paw and the sharp claw concealed under it in every society.[5]

Apparently, the writer could not conceive that a man would act so cavalierly toward a respectable Victorian woman. Hence, the author of the letter had to be another woman. How accurate was the assumption? Had a woman indeed written the letter? Certainly a woman in Adelaide's circle of acquaintances could have done so. Despite the earlier brouhaha at the Local Council, she was becoming something of a local heroine, especially as her reputation spread across the country. Under such circumstances, it was inevitable that she would have made enemies. But Adelaide's own personality must have increased the likelihood of there being those who wished her ill. She was, in the words of a contemporary, a woman who got things done. Indications are she had little patience with those who were slow to action. Furthermore, like many contemporary women, she considered herself morally upright. Having been shown the true way, in matters of religion and morality, it was her duty to point it out to others. And there is little doubt that Adelaide considered the teaching of domestic science morally right. She set herself up as an authority on all aspects of domesticity, and so she was bound to make enemies, particularly if she somehow conveyed the impression that her homemaking skills were superior to theirs. The wonder is that she did not have many more outspoken detractors, something that can only be explained by the fact that, despite an unswerving conviction in the correctness of her own views and methods, Adelaide possessed considerable charm, wit, and humour.

She also possessed persistence in abundance. Undeterred by the Board's refusal, and perhaps encouraged by the public display of support resulting from the Gordon letter, the YWCA committee submitted another proposal. This time, they offered "to equip and establish a Public School of Domestic Science"[6] in the Hunter Street building. It would run five afternoons a week, from January to the end of June, and the YWCA committee would pay the teacher's salary of $50 per month, plus expenses for material, fuel, and light. The Internal Management Committee looked into the matter, with some delegates visiting American trade schools during December. Early in January 1897, fully aware that the Ontario government was about to allow the teaching of domestic science in the province's schools, the Hamilton Board of Education accepted the YWCA's offer.

From the time that George Ross had accepted the idea of domestic science in the schools, he had apparently done everything possible to ensure the successful introduction of such courses in the province. The change in legislation did not make domestic science mandatory; it merely allowed the courses when desired by local school boards. What was needed now was a champion, a missionary to bring the gospel to the unconverted, and pave the way for compulsory domestic science education. And what better choice than the most outspoken advocate of domestic science, Adelaide Hoodless?

It is unclear precisely how the arrangement came about, or when. In a speech made in 1910, Adelaide told of fourteen years of campaigning for the Department of Education, carrying out her missionary work in Ontario towns and cities. That would indicate 1896 was the year she began to work as an unofficial representative of the government. If this were the case, it might help to explain the increasing lapses in diplomacy which crept into her arguments for domestic science. With the government behind her, she could sometimes afford to be blunt. So, for example, in a long letter to the editor of the *Spectator* , she wrote,

> In order that the question of domestic science in the public schools at present engaging the attention of educational authorities throughout Canada may be better understood by those who have not the time, or inclination, to study the matter, or whose lines have fallen in such pleasant places that they have not recognized any need for more scientific and intellectual influence bearing on home life.... The argument that the mother should train the daughters is simply twaddle.[7]

Despite such lapses, Adelaide was usually diplomatic in her handling of the school boards. Perhaps it was exasperation with the Hamilton Board which prompted her to word the letter strongly. In any event, she did her missionary work sufficiently well that, eventually, she would receive a token payment for it. On this basis, she is considered the first woman on the

Ontario provincial payroll, although her position was by no means a permanent one. But in 1896 there was no thought of payment, although Adelaide was already being asked to speak at educational institutions.

One such invitation brought her to the Ontario Agricultural College in Guelph in December 1896. The title of the speech she gave was 'The Relation of Domestic Science to the Agricultural Population.'' In her opening remarks, Adelaide said,

> When asked by your Secretary to give an outline of a course in Domestic Science suitbale for the Agricultural Population, I felt somewhat puzzled at first to know where to make a distinction between life in a country house and in that of a city home, as the actual needs must be very similar, and the same scientific training necessary.[8]

After referring to some of the work being undertaken in American manual training schools, Adelaide centred on the problems of a school system that did not take into consideration the unique situation of country people.

> The Public School system has sapped the rural districts of many of their brightest and most valuable members. Just so soon as a boy or girl discovers a special aptitude for text book work... they become convinced that their intellect is of the ''genius order'' and they are destined to shine as bright professional lights.[9]

It was a theme Adelaide had used before in an urban context, but this time she included variations of particular importance to the rural populace. She quoted an expert who claimed rural people had a higher rate of insanity, and argued that poor food, overwork, and monotony were contributing factors. The cure, of course , was obvious

> ... the causes are easily preventable... by Scientific knowledge of the various articles of food and their nutritive value, and ... by the introduction of schools of Domestic Science in the rural districts, with lecture courses and clubs for farmers' wives, where the better methods for producing good results in butter making, poultry raising, bee culture, house decoration, cookery, &c. may be intelligently discussed, thereby providing the best class of recreation, which is pleasure and and profit combined. The influence of the Agricultural College has been felt throughout the whole Province. Farmers are beginning to realize the importance of Scientific knowledge, that they must understand the chemistry of the Earth, the care of sheep, cattle and other live stock, the proper food required for certain climactic conditions, &c. and in consequence his work has become more attractive.... Now if this Scientific culture is so necessary for the development of farmers, is it not equally necessary for the farmer's wife, as we are told that it is not good to be ''unequally yoked''? Is it of greater importance that a farmer should know more about the Scientific care of his sheep and cattle, than that a farmer's wife should know how to care for her family, or that his barns should have every labor saving contrivance, while she toils and drudges on the same old treadmill instituted by her grandmother, perhaps even

to carrying water from a spring, a quarter of a mile from the house, which I know has been done— and providing the pies, hot cakes &c. which cause so much of the unrest and discontent in country homes.[10]

Adelaide continued, describing the County Councils in England and the Chautauqua School of Science, which provided what we would call continuing education for rural women. She also urged the establishment of a normal school in connection with the agricultural college. But it was her call for an organization for rural women which had the most far-reaching and immediate results. In the audience that day was Erland Lee, Secretary of the Farmer's Institutes. Inspired by her message, Lee would ask Adelaide to help establish such an organization.

Chapter Eight

Two New Organizations

Just as women were agitating for a variety of reforms, agriculture was in ferment in Canada. There was a growing awareness that farm productivity could be increased, given the right conditions. At the same time, farmers realized how important they were to the national economy, and banded together to wield their influence over the course of Canadian history. One organization which functioned in this capacity was the Farmer's Institute, established in Wentworth County in 1884.

Erland Lee, a young farmer from Stoney Creek, southeast of Hamilton, was one of the charter members of the Farmer's Institute. Like Adelaide, he was interested in education, for he had been a schoolteacher before receiving a certificate in agriculture from the Agriculture and Arts Association of Ontario. Like Adelaide, too, he was a dedicated reformer. He was 20 when he became involved in the Farmer's Institute, and he served as its secretary for nineteen years. In 1896, Lee was in charge of inviting speakers to Institute meetings, and, after hearing Adelaide speak, felt she should be an entertaining guest at the next Ladies' Night. He extended an invitation for the night of 12 February 1897.

Thirty-seven women were present that evening, and, during the course of her talk, Adelaide suggested they form an organization similar to the Farmer's Institute but not exclusively for women. The purpose of such an association, she explained, would not only be to broaden their knowledge of domestic science and agriculture, but also to bring women together to socialize. "Life on a farm can be pretty dull and lonely," she said. "I know, I was brought up on one."[1]

It is possible that Erland Lee had suggested the structure of the women's organization in conversation with Adelaide prior to the meeting. Perhaps the idea simply evolved out of general discussion during the meeting, especially if Lee repeated the remarks Adelaide had made at the Ontario Agricultural College. Whatever the case, the idea seemed a good one, and when Lee asked if Adelaide would return to talk to the women about such an organization the following week, she agreed.

During the next several days, Lee and his wife Janet, who had also been a teacher and shared his enthusiasm for progress, travelled around Saltfleet Township, calling on women and asking them to come to the meeting. As prominent members of the community, the Lees were able to convince many women to come and hear Adelaide speak. Curiosity must have played a part, too, for Adelaide's name was well-known through newspaper accounts of her activities. Furthermore, as an extra attraction, Adelaide was bringing a guest with her, Mrs. Rorer, author of a popular cookbook and principal of a Toronto cooking school.

Bernard Hoodless later recalled that night.

> It was my privilege as a boy to hitch up her favorite horse, Scotty, and drive her down to Stoney Creek on that stormy night of February 19, 1897. I can still remember that meeting in the old hall, up a rickety flight of outside stairs, and sliding into a seat at the back and wondering what it was all about. [2]

One hundred and one women, as well as Erland Lee, had gathered at Squire's Hall that night. By the time the evening was over, they had formed the Department of Domestic Economy in affiliation with the Farmer's Institute, to be called the Women's Department of the Farmer's Institute of South Wentworth.'' [3] The following week, at the first formal meeting of the organization, the name was changed to the Women's Institute of Saltfleet Township.

Erland Lee proposed a constitution, which Janet had written out on their dining room table.

> The object of this Institute shall be to promote that knowledge of household science which shall lead to the improvement in household architecture with special attention to home sanitation, to a better understanding of economics and hygiene value of foods and fuels, and to a more scientific care of children with a view to raising the general standards of our people. [4]

At the February 25th, meeting, which was held at the home of E. D. Smith, the executive of the organization was elected. Mrs. E. D. Smith was made president, Mrs. Melson vice-president, and Janet Lee was a director. Adelaide became honourary president. The Institute established six areas of interest: domestic economy; architecture, with a special reference to heat, light, sanitation, and ventilation; health, including physiology, hygiene, calisthenics and medicine; floriculture and horticulture; music and art; literature, education, sociology, and legislation.

Although the Women's Institute was an organization with its own executive and its own goals, it remained affiliated with the Farmer's Institute, for very good reasons. Almost as soon as it was founded, Erland Lee sought government support for the Institute. He wrote to W. F. Hodson, Superintendent of the Farmer's Institutes, asking for his help in having the Women's Institute granted a charter under the Agricultural Societies Act. This would be granted in 1902, but, in the meantime, the Women's Institute would flourish under the protection of its stronger brother organization.

As usual at nineteenth-century organizational meetings, papers were read at the Women's Institute gatherings. At the first meeting, the two topics were ''Proper Food for Children'' and ''Art.'' By the end of the year, Stoney Creek could boast seventy-five members, and soon a second

Institute was established at Whitby.

During the first year, the average attendance was about sixty women per meeting, and when a subject of particular interest to women was discussed, the doors were locked to prevent unwelcome male intrusions. It is reasonable to assume that, in addition to offering information on the latest techniques which could be applied to the running of a farm and home, the Women's Institute functioned as a self-help group, where women who were isolated for long periods of time could get together with others in similar circumstances, discuss various problems, and seek solutions and moral support.

The Women's Institute was a major force in the education of rural women. Because of government involvement, the members benefited from the knowledge of various experts who travelled to meetings at government expense. But Adelaide made it clear from the outset that theoretical knowledge would never be enough on its own. To hold the Women's Institutes together we must send them trained instructors, not merely high in book learning, but clear-headed active women who can go into the garden... and destroy insect pests; women who can perform with their own hands the work of butter making, cooking etc., instructors who can show how to do a thing.[5] She also spoke of the goal of the Women's Institute in relation to rural women. ''We must educate them... the Agricultural College at Guelph must throw open to young women on the same terms as to young men.''[6] In making this statement, Adelaide was prophesying the future of the Women's Institute and domestic science education.

One of the first government employees to speak at the Women's Institutes was Laura Rose, who taught dairying at the Ontario Agricultural College. She was the epitome of the kind of woman Adelaide wanted for the Women's Institute. Born in Georgetown, as a teenager she had been her brother's housekeeper on a North Dakota farm for a time . To supplement the household income, she had also taught school during the same period. After returning to Ontario, she enrolled in the Farm Dairy School at the OAC, graduated with honours, and was hired as an instructor, a position she held for thirteen years. Laura also wrote articles for farm journals, as well as a textbook, *Farm Dairying*, which was used in several agricultural schools. She was a popular speaker at the Women's Institutes, ''A fluent, instructive and entertaining speaker, and possessing an amiable and charming personality.''[7] In addition to establishing the second Women's Institute in Canada at Whitby, she also deserves much of the credit for turning Adelaide's idea of an organization into a flourishing reality.

While Adelaide Hoodless has long been credited with founding the Women's Institute, and the membership of that organization has done more than any other to keep her memory alive, she was only peripherally involved in Institute work. From time to time she attended meetings, such as one on 26 January 1899, when she urged the Institute to affiliate with the National Council of Women. For the most part, however, Adelaide left the Women's Institute in the capable hands of rural women, while she continued her campaign for domestic science in towns and cities.

In the same year, which, coincidentally was the year of Queen Victoria's second jubilee, Adelaide also played a small part in creating an organization which would continue to flourish nine decades later, the Victorian Order of Nurses.

At the National Council of Women meeting in 1896, Lady Aberdeen suggested there was a national need for visiting nurses, women who could care for the sick in remote areas, where doctors were rare or non-existent. Adelaide quickly became involved in the proposed organization. Her interest in these district nurses, as they were called, was understandable, since part of their duties would be housekeeping and preparing food suitable for invalids. One can almost see her arguing that a comprehensive course in domestic science would have to be part of the nurses' training. Certainly any arguments along these lines would have been justified, for the nurses, in effect, would have to practice domestic science as well as the healing arts.

Quite likely Lady Aberdeen actively sought Adelaide's help in establishing the VON. Already, Adelaide had a reputation for getting things done, and she seems to have had a knack for raising funds. Her presence in any group greatly increased the chances of tasks being carried out successfully.

On 15 January 1897, a committee was appointed to consider the establishment of an order of visiting district nurses. The committee had English precedents on which to base the Canadian project. Dr. Albert Napper, a British doctor, had started cottage hospitals in England in 1857 to provide health care for patients beyond the reach of the larger hospitals. In 1887, an organization of visiting nurses had been formed under the patronage of Queen Victoria. Lady Aberdeen hoped the Canadian order could be formed along similar lines.

On Febraury 2nd, the *Ottawa Citizen* ran an article describing the plans of Lady Aberdeen and her husband, who wholeheartedly supported the scheme. The next day, a small medical advisory commitee held their first meeting, at which tentative plans for the selection and training of nurses was drawn up. A week later, at an open meeting in Ottawa, Wilfred Laurier formally proposed the formation of the Victoria Order of Home Helpers. It was decided that an organizing committee should approach the Queen for her approval of the organization which was to be named in her honour.

Five days later, an official statement issued from Government House detailed the plans of the Victorian Order, including eligibility. In addition to thorough training, the nurses should be mature women of at least twenty-eight. Preference would be given to women who already lived in country districts and were respected by their neighbours.

By this time, the prime minister had more or less promised that the government would vote a large sum of money to the order. Queen Victoria's official sanction was expected shortly, and it seemed that the organization was off to a wonderful start. But, almost immediately after the publication of the official announcement, a controversy erupted.

Somehow, an impression had been created that the VON nurses would be inadequately trained, and that they would replace doctors in remote districts. The medical community objected, seeing the nurses as a threat to their pocketbooks as well as the patients' health. One of the most vocal opponent of the VON was Sir Charles Tupper, a medical doctor who had been prime minister of Canada for two months in 1896. Tupper took out advertisements in several newspapers warning readers to stay clear of "these female quacks" and predicting that they could only ruin the practice of country doctors.

The Ontario Medical Council also opposed the project. So violent was the feeling against the Order, in fact, that friends urged Lady Aberdeen to abandon the project, claiming it would cause bad feelings between Canadians and the vice-regal couple.

Undeterred, Lady Aberdeen continued her campaign, and enlisted the help of Dr. Alfred Worcester, founder of the Waltham Training School near Boston, Massachusetts.

Worcester readily admitted that the Waltham School had been based on Florence Nightingale's ideas and the Jubilee nurses, the British order of visiting nurses. He felt it was important, therefore, to repay his debt to Britain by aiding Canada. As a result, he spoke to Ottawa doctors of the benefits of district nurses, and, with little difficulty, persuaded them to support the VON. Toronto doctors proved far less co-operative.

Several hundred Toronto doctors were invited to hear Dr. Worcester speak at At. George's Hall. Two hundred showed up, and while they enjoyed the food and drink provided for them, they were not particularly pleased with Worcester. In fact, they were extremely rude, ignoring him while he spoke, carrying on private conversations, and eventually peppering him with some extremely nasty questions and remarks. Worcester parried as best he could, insisting that it was his professional duty to inform his colleagues of the benefit visiting nurses could bring to patients.

The doctors remained unconvinced. Finally, someone made a slighting reference to the Queen and her patronage of the order. Worcester, an American, was quick to defend the British sovereign. Ironically, it was this action which turned the tables in his favour. Impressed with his gallantry, several doctors invited him to their private club. They talked long into the night, and Worcester felt he was making headway. What really underscored his success was a newspaper article reporting on his defence of the Queen. Popular sympathy turned in favour of Worcester, and, ultimately, in favour of the Victorian Order. Not long afterward, the Ontario Medical Association endorsed the scheme.

Adelaide's contribution to the Victorian Order of Nurses was peripheral during these early critical days, yet her involvement in the scheme cannot be overlooked. In December 1898, she was involved in a public meeting in Hamilton, at which the purpose of the Order was decribed. As in Ottawa and Toronto, there was opposition to the scheme, with only one doctor and a few nurses giving any encouragement. However, inspired by the example of other cities, the organizers worked steadily towards their goal of bringing the VON to Hamilton.

On 8 March 1899, the first recorded meeting of the executive meeting of the Hamilton branch of the VON took place. Among the people in attendance were the Honourable William Elie Sanford, former Mayor of Hamilton, Benjamin Charlton, and their wives. Adelaide also attended. As a result, the Hamilton group sent a formal request to the national Board of Governors asking permission to establish a branch of the VON in Hamilton.

Charlotte MacLeod, the Order's "lady superintendent" visited the city to speak on the benefits the nurses could provide. By May, a board of management had been established, whose job would be managing the branch and any nurses attached to it. And, on 26 July, the first VON nurse, Emily Daken, reached Hamilton. Almost immediately after her arrival, she was put to work, and, over the next decade and a half, three more nurses would join the Hamilton branch.

In spite of these accomplishments, the VON occupied only a small portion of Adelaide's energies. While her standing in the community undoubtedly helped sway public opinion in favour of the VON, she was much too deeply involved in domestic science to take a major role in the organization of a branch of visiting nurses.

Adelaide Hoodless.

Chapter Nine

The Little Red Book

While helping to establish the VON and the Women's Institute, Adelaide was deeply involved with domestic science education. In June 1897, the *Hamilton Times* reported on the commencement exercises of the school of domestic science. The ceremony took place in the basement of the public library, with Adelaide officiating. According to the newspaper report,

> Mrs. Hoodless told of the progress made by domestic science in leading educational centres of the old land, where it had become almost as strongly established a feature of Public School training as any of the time-honoured three R's, referred to the prominent position accorded to it in certain of the Public schools of the United States, and then described the varying successes it met with in Canada in the efforts to have the girls and young women of today taught, in a scientific way, how to be good homemakers and home keepers. [1]

Adelaide gave an account of the success of the past school year, the second for the YWCA school of domestic science.

> We started with 94 pupils, of which 15 moved away during the term, nine left school entirely, and 63 remained for the final lessons. Of the latter number, all tried the examination in Domestic Science, in addition to the work of their ordinary midsummer examinations, and 48 passed. [2]

Some of the girls won prizes for cooking and breadmaking as well. Adelaide also spoke of her hopes for a Normal School in Hamilton as a special project to celebrate Queen Victoria's jubilee. ''The speaker had hoped this college might have been made the Jubilee building of the city this year, but the powers that be thought differently.''[3] With an obviously sympathetic audience listening to her opinions, Adelaide took the opportunity to reiterate the objections the local Board of Education had made to the introduction of domestic science. Apparently, her views were gaining ground, for a little later in the evening, when one of the dignitaries attending the ceremony said he felt the Board of Education might possibly extend domestic science courses in the schools, there was warm applause.

From the Board of Education's viewpoint, the prime objection to domestic science classes was financial. The Board was well aware that any move which raised taxes would meet with objections from some quarters. Yet that argument was often accompanied by criticism of domestic science education as worthless. More and more, however, it was becoming apparent that this was just not so.

It may be an open question whether instruction in domestic science should be given at the public expense. But it cannot be successfully shown that such training should not be given because the results are not satisfactory.[4]

The results, in fact, were eminently satisfactory, and partly because of them Adelaide was invited to speak on various occasions in Hamilton and outside the city. One place she appeared in 1897 was the Southern Fair in Brantford, where she talked on domestic science. Along with her usual persuasive arguments on the topic, Adelaide announced that the first examinations for teachers of the subject had been held in Toronto, Ottawa, and Hamilton on July 6th and 7th, an event which pointed to growing official support for the subject. Although Adelaide's remarks were well received by some of her listeners, and hope was expressed that Brantford would introduce domestic science in its public schools, several listeners were alienated by one tactless comment.

> Mrs. Hoodless ventured the assertion that no more than two scientifically constructed, really wholesome loaves of bread were in the exhibit, and said that the hardest thing in the world is to convince a woman that she cannot make good bread.[5]

If the report was accurate, it shows a definite tendency on Adelaide's part to throw diplomacy out the window when stressing the merits of domestic science. It is also ironic that she chooses to make such a statement in the Brantford area. Her birthplace was nearby, and it is conceivable that some of her listeners knew her ''way back when'' and did not take kindly to her self-endowed authority on domestic matters.

However, despite setbacks and the occasional *faux pas* , Adelaide was increasingly aware of the progress she was making towards her chosen goal. A further sign of this progress was the assignment, given to her by the Ministry of Education, to prepare a textbook for use in domestic science courses. Titled *Public School Domestic Science* , the book was published by Copp Clark in 1898.

''The little red book'', as it was nicknamed, contained some straightforward advice on the teaching of cooking in public schools. ''Owing to the limited time allowed for this course in the Public Schools, it will be impossible to teach more than a few of the first principles,''[6] Adelaide explained at the outset. She stressed the importance of hygiene as an integral part of the curriculum:

> Personal cleanliness must be insisted upon. Special attention should be given to the hands and nails. The hair should be carefully pinned back or confined in some way, and covered by a cap.... Untidy habits must not be allowed in the classroom. Set an example of perfect order and neatness, and insist upon pupils following that example. Teach the pupils that cooking may be done without soiling either the hands or clothes.

> The pupils should do all the work of the classroom, except scrubbing the floor. Everything must be left in perfect order at the close of each lesson. [7]

She also stressed frugality:

> It is a great mistake to think that the best is [not] the cheapest in regard to the food question, that the higher priced meats, fish, butter, etc. contain special virtues lacking in the cheaper articles. Poor cooking is the chief cause of this error in judgement. [8]

The text offered a couple of options in terms of course content, depending on the time available to the teacher. The shorter version included an introductory lesson on firemaking, personal cleanliness and measuring, followed by lessons covering:

1. A cereal and a fruit.
2. Eggs.
3. Bacon, and the frying out of fat.
4. Plain muffins, or griddle cakes. Coffee.
5. A breakfast.
6. Vegetables. Vegetable soup.
7. A made dish of meat or fish.
8. Salad and dressing.
9. Muffins or biscuits.
10. A luncheon or supper.
11. Vegetables. Macaroni.
12. Meat.
13. Sauces and gravies. A dessert.
14. Bread or rolls.
15. A dinner. [9]

The text not only included recipes donated by the Councils of Women across the country, and cooking techniques, but dwelt on kitchen equipment and economical shopping practices. Seasonal recipes were given, including recipes which could be made without eggs, especially useful for the winter, when, Adelaide noted, ''eggs are dear.''[10]

Adelaide provided plenty of information on food chenistry as it was understood at the time, meat charts, and advice on selecting the best and freshest foods. ''The best chickens have soft yellow feet, short thick legs, smooth moist skin and plump breast:... Pin feathers always indicate a young bird and long hairs an older one.''[11] Much of the material she included was derivative, however, based on existing references on the subject. Adelaide's lack of formal domestic science training was something of an obstacle: by the time the second edition of the text was being prepared, Mary Urie Watson, graduate of a university domestic science course, had been made co-author.

Still, the first textbook for Canadian schools was a valiant effort, even if it did reveal as much of Adelaide's character as her beliefs in what constituted good household practices. Inevitably, considering the tragic loss of John Harold, she focused on hygiene in the section on nursing bottles and feeding.

> Have two plain bottles with rubber tops, without tubes. Bottles with ounces and tablespoons marked on them, can be purchased and are a great convenience in measuring the amount of food required. After using the bottle, empty the remaining milk; rinse in cold water, then in scalding water. If particles of milk adhere to the bottle use coarse salt or raw potato cut in small pieces. If the glass looks cloudy, add a little ammonia to the water. Turn the rubber tops inside out and scrub with a stiff brush; boil them every alternate day for 10 minutes. *Absolute cleanliness is a necessity* in the care of baby's food, bottles and rubber tops.[12]

As befitting the author of a text on domestic science, Adelaide included various generalized tips on homemaking in her "Suggestions for young housekeepers."

> Carefully supervise the daily dietary so that a reasonable proportion of the necessary food elements may be provided. See that the proportion of protein is one part to four of carbohydrates and fats. Adapt the dietary to the season and climate. Do not waste time and money in preparing rich puddings, entrées, cakes, etc., when fresh fruit, vegetables, salads, etc. are so much more nutritious, economical, and convenient. Arrange to have a variety of foods — different kinds of meat, fish and poultry, — cooked in various ways. See that suitable food is provided the children; especially pure milk and food containing mineral salts. Do not allow children to use tea, coffee, or other stimulants. A glass of hot milk (not boiled) is the best stimulant for a child when wearied with study or over exertion of any kind. See that water which has stood in the pipes over night is drawn before filling the tea-kettle for breakfast, or using the water for porridge or other purposes. Rinse the tea-kettle every morning before using. Never use water from the hot tank for cooking. See that the water used for drinking purposes is pure; if suspicious, either have it filtered or boiled before using. Do not allow soiled rags, dish cloths or towels to lie around the kitchen. Wash and scald the dish cloths and towels after each dish washing, hanging them outside to dry — if possible. Keep plenty of clean towels; some fine ones for glass and china, coarser ones for general use. Keep a holder within reach of the oven so as to avoid burning the fingers, or using an apron. See that a kettleful of boiling water is poured down the sink pipes every day. All boxes, jars and shelves in which food is kept, must be kept scrupulously clean and well aired. The refrigerator requires special attention; see that the drain pipe and interior of the ice box are kept thoroughly clean. A stiff wire with a piece of cloth fastened on the end may be used to clean the drain pipe at least once a week. Do not have any closet under the sink or places of concealment for dirty pots and pans....[13]

One thing which emerged in the textbook was Adelaide's obsession with cleanliness. This preoccupation sometimes had inadvertently amusing results, as she carried her cleanliness campaign into all aspects of her life. She travelled frequently as a result of her work, and thus it must have been as a result of her own shocked sensibilities that she persuaded the Hamilton Local Council of Women to urge railway companies to upgrade their standards of cleanliness.

According to one report of the Local Council,

> Mrs. Hoodless gave a resumé of her efforts concerning sanitary conditions in railway stations and coaches, one of the many reforms for which she labored. She had interviewed prominent railway officials of both the Canadian Pacific and Grand Trunk Railways, who had assured her of their hearty co-operation. It was made clear in her report that the travelling public needed education in sanitary protection quite as much, if not more, than the railway companies. The selfishness displayed by some women in not only occupying the toilet room an unreasonable length of time, but in leaving it in a most untidy condition should be prevented in some way. The report recommended that a notice be posted in all toilet rooms, requesting passengers to leave the basins, etc., in such conditions as they would wish to find them; that a fair amount of time should be allowed each passenger for dressing. The report recommended that all large stations should be scrubbed every night, and smaller ones at least once a week; all seats and window ledges to be cleaned daily. A suitable disinfectant should be used every day in all basins and lavatories, proper ventilation afforded in all waiting rooms and passenger coaches; a receptacle should be provided in all stations and coaches for waste paper and other refuse. Spitting on the floor should be a punishable offence. Passengers should make it their business to report unclean coaches, lavatories, etc. to the proper authorities. It was believed that only by the co-operation of the travelling public and the railway companies could better sanitary conditions be secured. Mrs. Hoodless also advocated the use of individual paper drinking cups.[14]

Whether in her own home, in domestic science classes, or on the train, Adelaide never forgot the high standards of cleanliness she felt were an integral part of the homemaker's role.

Chapter Ten

Conquest by Charm

The beginning of 1898 brought a setback for the cause of domestic science in Hamilton. At a meeting of the Board of Education held on January 6th, the Domestic Science Sub-committee recommended the acceptance of the YWCA's offer to furnish accommodations and a teacher to the public school pupils until July 1st. The cost to the Board would be $400, which worked out to $8 per student.

There was considerable discussion among the members of the Board regarding this offer. One major objection brought forward was that domestic science education was not reaching the students who would benefit most. "Only the better class of pupils were getting the advantage and the girls who needed it most could not get the training." [1] As a result of the debate, the Sub-committee's recommendation was defeated by a vote of six to five. Domestic science classes for public school students would end.

Adelaide could not let the matter drop without a struggle. On January 8th, her letter to the editor of the *Hamilton Times* discussed the issue. After criticizing members of the Board of Education for ignorance and shortsightedness, she asked,

> Why should any Trustee say whether the teaching of Domestic Science is more suitable for the poor than the rich? After five years experience with all classes I unhesitatingly say that the children of the poor know quite as much as the children of the rich. Are not the interests of the two so intermingled that what is good for one is good for the other? [2]

One wonders if the remark on similar levels of knowledge in both groups was meant to be an ironic comment on a common lack of information. Certainly the rhetorical question on intermingled interests reflected a rather simplistic view of Canadian class structures. Did Adelaide envision an educated upper class spreading their domestic science knowledge to the less fortunate in subsequent generations, either through work such as that carried out by the YWCA school of domestic science, or through the training of servants by educated chatelaines? Or was she thinking of highly trained domestic help by improving conditions in upper class homes?

Far less ambiguous was her attack on the criticism that led to the cancellation of the arrangements with the Board.

> It was stated as one reason for the termination of the classes "that the class for whom they were provided had not availed themselves of the privilege." Whose fault is this? When over 600 applied from the various

Public schools for such instruction, the members of the board concluded that as accomodation could only be provided for a limited number, the only way by which they could solve the difficulty was to confine the teaching to the commercial form.[3]

A third of the letter was a treatise on the value of domestic science programmes and their implementation in other countries. It was the last paragraph of the letter, however, which likely stirred most interest among its readers:

> ...are these gentlemen aware that domestic science has already been added to the Public School curriculum by the Department of Education and that it is only a question of time until it becomes a compulsory subject? Are we to lose the reputation attained by our city for its progressive spirit in educational matters simply because a few men oppose the introduction of a valuable subject— who have not taken the time or trouble... to pay even one visit to the classes since last September in order to see for themselves what is being taught, who state that these classes interfere with the regular school work, notwithstanding the fact that head masters have publicly stated to the contrary?[4]

Adelaide's appeal to Hamiltonians' pride in progress was undoubtedly aided by the fact that the domestic science courses were gaining popularity. In response to another critical letter, one of the domestic science students wrote:

> In reply to the letter of A Mother, I would like to say that she has not had correct information concerning domestic science. In the term just past, 157 girls attended the classes. I have attended for nearly a year and a half. If any of the girls had wished they could have stopped, but they all enjoyed the time spent and profited by it. Each girl had her work to do and do properly, and if any girls calls that "fun" there is no more to be raised than if she called any other subject she likes "fun." As for cooking expensive things, we learned how to cook meat and vegetables properly, and how to make good bread, besides many other things useful to us. I hear a great many speak in favor of its adoption, as I know a large number of girls attending the classes and their parents as well as the girls wish it carried on. If there is too much cramming in the schools let some of the less useful subjects be dropped in favor of domestic science which any unprejudiced person cannot help seeing is greatly beneficial, to the homes and general welfare of the scholars. I would not ask Mrs. Hoodless to stay at home any more than she does, as she is there plenty long enough to attend to her "affairs" and attend to them properly, too, and as for the "mother" thinking Mrs. Hoodless can learn by so doing, she ought to find out for certain before saying any such thing, as she is entirely mistaken, because there is no branch of domestic science on which Mrs. Hoodless cannot give information, and she deserves great credit for the part she has taken in forwarding domestic science and she has my best wishes for success. One of the girls[5]

Such evidence of support for the programme and her methods must have been tremendously encouraging to Adelaide. Still, something more was required to prove that domestic science had the support of the public — or at least that segment of the public which was informed of its aims. To do this, Adelaide sent out questionnaires to the parents of the girls enrolled in the domestic science courses. The questions were:

> Has the time given to the domestic science classes seriously interfered with other school work? Do you consider the subject of sufficient importance to counterbalance the time taken from other subjects, or do you consider the time wasted? Has your daughter made satisfactory progress? Has she practiced the lessons at home? Would you be in favor of all girls attending the senior grades receiving instruction in Domestic Science?[6]

More than one hundred replies were received, and of these, only one demonstrated dissatisfaction with the courses, Adelaide reported. Armed with this and other proofs of support, she and the YWCA attempted to convince the Board of Education to extend the courses in domestic science yet again.

While the Board deliberated, Adelaide travelled to a meeting of the National Council in May to talk of the impact of domestic science education. One of her remarks was particularly revealing.

> As to the influence of university education for women little can as yet be said. But no amount of intellectuality can compensate for the absence of that loving and unselfish consideration of others which is woman's greatest charm.[7]

In light of her later clashes with university-trained experts in domestic science, it is probable that Adelaide had considerable suspicion of women with superior academic training, and, possibly, was convinced that university was not necessary for women, the majority of whom were more likely to need a good grounding in domestic science.

By the end of June, the domestic science courses were irrevocably cancelled, the Board of Education being of the opinion that such courses, if taught at all, should be taught within the regular school programme. A consequence of this cancellation was considerable speculation about the worth of the subject.

By July, Adelaide deemed it expedient to resolve the matter once and for all. She wrote a letter to the Board of Education.

> The action of the Board of Education in dealing with the question of domestic science in the public schools, has either been misrepresented through the newspapers, or a serious injustice has been committed by

the board.... several letters have been received from those who are interested in the question of practical education in other cities and towns throughout the province, asking, ''why the board decided against its introduction into the schools'' and ''if the experiment proved a failure?'' and in every case containing such expressions as the following, which is an extract from the letter of a leading educationalist, ''I hope the decision of the board was not final, as Hamilton has been considered the pioneer in this work. The report, as given by the newspapers, is certainly condemnatory. Please give me the facts concerning the matter.'' ...through the inaction of the Board of Education, without even asking for a report, the subject has been condemned and the public allowed to receive the false impression that the experiment has been a failure.... If the Board of Education had expressed its satisfaction with the experimental test, and reported such fact to the education department, at the same time declining to take further action in the matter until the curriculum be re-adjusted and proper provision made for its introduction? Such action would have been satisfactory to all concerned, and given the department some idea of public opinion regarding the matter.... It does seem plausible that the Hamilton board could have known the far-reaching effect of its apparent injustice to a good cause, and on behalf of those interested in the subject, I ask the board if it will kindly correct this false impression through the press.[8]

It took several weeks for the Board to respond, probably due to delays brought about by summer vacations. A. M. McPherson, chairman of the Internal Management Committee, finally wrote,

From a communication received from Mrs. Hoodless it appears that an erroneous impression has gone abroad respecting the action of the Board upon the subject of teaching Domestic Science in the Public Schools. The facts are that on the 14th of January 1897 at the request of a number of ladies connected with the Young Women's Christian Association, the Board agreed to contribute a certain amount to that institution towards paying the salary of a duly qualified teacher, in return for which a limited number of senior fourth and public school leaving pupils from the Public Schools received instruction from the instituttion referred to in Domestic Science for a specified time. This arrangment was, at the request of the ladies referred to, continued for a further period and then terminated, the Board being of the opinion that Domestic Science, if taught at all, should be included in the regular school curriculum and form part of the Public school studies. It may be added further that the arrangement above alluded to was not terminated either because the Board was adverse to instruction being given in Domestic Science, or because the arrangment alluded to was of an unsatisfactory nature.[9]

In addition to the vindication provided by the Board of Education's letter, Adelaide had another reason to feel triumphant. At the end of October, the Kingston YWCA opened a domestic science school similar to the Hamilton establishment. Adelaide talked to the guests who attended the formal opening. Along with the inevitable praise of domestic science education, local papers reported, "she believed in the YWCA throwing out its book-keeping and type-writing classes and go in for instruction in domestic duties."[10] Adelaide also apparently noted at this time that men were more sympathetic to domestic science than women. Her own experience had certainly borne this out, since her harshest critics were invariably women, possibly because many of Adelaide's statements on the ignorance of the average homemaker could easily be interpreted as threatening.

By this time Adelaide was increasingly convinced that domestic science would soon be an integral part of the course of studies in Ontario schools, although, contrary to her newspaper statement, it was not yet a regular part of the school curricula. However, this move was being contemplated, and Adelaide was convinced it would take place very soon. An important chapter in her life, the lengthy battle to convince the provincial Department of Education to allow domestic science in public schools, was drawing to a close.

There was another ending as well that year. the Aberdeens were returning to Britain, partly because of illness in the family, but also because the controversy which surrounded them had grown to unmanageable proportions. From Quebec City, Lady Aberdeen wrote Adelaide a short note,

> Dear Mrs. Hoodless,
>
> May I ask you acceptance of a tiny souvenir of your first National Council President, who will always remember with true appreciation the wonderful kindness and loyalty of her colleagues and fellow workers in Canada.
> I shall not easily forget that conversation with you which led to my becoming President, nor all the common work we have endeavoured to carry out together since that time.
> May you greatly prosper in your present undertaking, and if I can ever help you, please let me know.
>
> Beleive me,
> Yours Sincerely,
> Ishbel Aberdeen.[11]

Adelaide had little time to regret Lady Aberdeen's departure, for her own star was rising. As support for domestic science increased, Adelaide was no longer considered an eccentric, fighting against the mainstream of educational theory. Instead, she was regarded as an expert in her own right, and a charming one at that.

Contemporary reports made much of her gifts as a speaker. She possessed a "rare mental endowment, having a facile gift for oral exposition."[12] She was a handsome woman, with the full, large-bosomed figure so admired at the time, a fact which was frequently remarked upon by the papers: "a pleasant faced magnetic speaker."[13] She also gained a reputation for wit, warmth, and enthusiasm. "Mrs. Hoodless is a convincing lecturer. In addition to her charming manner, she carries weight by her intense enthusiasm."[14] She had "the happy faculty of carrying her hearers with her enthusiasm for the subject, and the practical common sense she displays in its presentation."[15] Yet, even as she spoke on her area of expertise, she minimized her own achievements. Speaking to a high school convocation in Orangeville, she called herself "a plain, unpretentious woman."[16]

One of the reasons Adelaide held her audiences' attention was her sense of humour. She apparently loved to laugh and was not above sharing a joke with her listeners, especially if it made a point. When discussing the lack of housekeeping skills in Canadian homes, for example, she told a Belleville audience, "A lady went into a butcher shop in Hamilton the other day and instead of asking for a piece of veal asked for the side of a calf."[17]

But it was her message which was most important, and Adelaide never tired of delivering it. During the course of her career, she made hundreds, perhaps thousands of speeches on domestic science. After she was appointed to speak for the Ontario government on the subject, the frequency of her public appearances increased to the point where she might be speaking in four or more different towns within a single week.

In addition to outlining the kind of domestic science programmes needed in Ontario schools, Adelaide talked of her own beliefs and some of the problems she had experienced. She generally began her talk by defining the terms of reference. Again and again she explained that domestic science was not cooking, but modern education. "Domestic science teaches how to prepare food, and it deals with the economy of time and money."[18] "The word domestic science implies home science, the art of home making, and the subject is taught from the standpoint of economics."[19] Adelaide wanted the subject introduced in kindergarten, with cooking classes to begin when students reached the age of 12. In her opinion, it was never too early to begin to prepare girls for their roles as mothers and homemakers.

For those who remained unconvinced, she offered a persuasive argument.

> There is a standard for everything else. Why should there not be an education standard for homemakers? We exact a certain standard from our teachers, our physicians, our clergymen; we see that they spend the necessary time in properly educating and fitting themselves for their life work. Why should we not do the same in homemaking?[20]

Experience, if not her own innate common sense, had taught Adelaide that a few projects turned out precisely as planned. Furthermore, she was well aware of the achingly slow speed at which bureaucracies operated, especially when introducing any new programme. So, when she appeared before audiences who might work towards the introduction of domestic science, she passed on her own experiences and advice. The *Berlin News Record*, for example, reported on her efforts to amass the best equipment possible for Canadian schools, as well as Adelaide's philosophical assessment of her chances of reaching ther goal. ''Aim at an electric light and you may get a gas jet,''[21] she said.

While women were appearing on the platform more than they had at the outset of Adelaide's career, partly due to the example set by Lady Aberdeen, they were still in the minority. A lingering doubt remained in the minds of many that any woman in such a prominent position was not quite respectable. Perhaps because of this, as well as the fact that it was basically good advertising for her domestic science crusade, Adelaide frequently discussed her own beliefs regarding the place of woman in society, beliefs that were frequently at odds with those held by some of the most progressive women of the day.

> She iterated and reiterated her belief that the wife and mother who watches and helps in the education of her children and makes home bright and sweet for the family and her friends is doing better work for humanity than those who wish to assume the duties of men.[22]

In fact, Adelaide frequently pointed to the deterioration of home life as one of the causes for immorality, the rising crime rate, and the increase in divorces. In one address, she decried a society where ''men are making a god of the mighty dollar and women making a god of dress and ostentatious display.''[23] and, when she spoke to young women at Pittsburgh's Carnegie Institute the same year, she told them that education in household science was the best guarantee against divorce.

''It is just as much a woman's place to furnish a happy home as it is a man's to provide the bread and butter,'' Adelaide remarked on another occasion,

> When young women and older ones too for that matter, cease to look upon the work of keeping house as a menial and distasteful task and regard it in the light of an occupation or profession from the lowest to highest rounds, there will be fewer divorces asked for and granted.[24]

While her ideas were still considered somewhat radical, Adelaide repeatedly stated her opposition to the suffrage movement.

> Woman has had, from creation, distinctly designed duties, and until the power of education and influence is brought to bear upon these duties, and she has demonstrated her ability to do her own work well, she has no right to infringe on man's perogative.[25]

In fact, Adelaide was convinced there was no need for women to vote. ''Good men have never denied the women of this country anything they have gone about getting in the right way,''[26] she told a Cleveland audience in 1904.

Adelaide, family and friends on an outing at Grimsby, ca. 1906.

Because of her celebrity, Adelaide's opinion was sought on many matters. She often attributed her success to a higher source:

> Providence has seen fit to use me as an agent in the cause of domestic education, and my success is due entirely to my belief in his guidance and power to make all things work for good.[27]

However, she was still quite willing to voice her opinion, particularly when asked to describe a well-rounded life.

> I... believe in the benefit of a more liberal social life through cooperation in work of social and educational reform. I also believe in the necessity of recreation among women in order to produce all-round knowledge and sympathy with social conditions. I find a game of golf one of the most stimulating and healthful amusements possible for strengthening of brain and nerve power[28]

Adelaide belonged to two clubs, in fact, the Hamilton Golf Club and the Toronto Club. she also enjoyed bridge, probably as much for the opportunities to socialize it provided as for the game itself. It is also likely, like many Victorians, she enjoyed wine and spirits.

Somehow, she managed to balance her demanding work schedule with an equally demanding social life. One of her daughters recalled,

> Mother had travelled widely and there were always interesting people coming and going.... She had a stimulating and loving personality that drew young and old alike. Yet she seemed to have time for everything. She used to say, ''Women must learn not to waste valuable time on non-essentials,'' and I think much of her success was due to her wise choice of essentials and concentration on same.[29]

Yet she still had many critics. In some areas of the province, Adelaide was definitely not welcome. Eastern Ontario in particular expressed little interest in having her visit, seemingly because Ottawa already had a flouishing school of domestic science. But Adelaide was determined to bring Eastern Ontario, especially the national capital, within her sphere of influence, even if it meant defying the Department of Education.

Just before one trip to Ottawa, Richard Harcourt wrote a hurried letter to Adelaide

> I have a letter from Ottawa insisting that you shall not go there, that if you were to go your visit would do harm, that your last visit set the cause back, etc., etc. It seems that all arrangements are being made as we would wish them. You had better delay your visit therefore until I have time to talk the matter over with you....[30]

The letter was written on 14 March 1902, and reached Eastcourt the following day. But Adelaide was already in Belleville, unknown to Harcourt, who sent a telegram to her at home. ''Carry out plan other than as relates to Ottawa.''[31] Edna wired back that she had forwarded the telegram to her mother. Whether Adelaide received it in time or not, she decided to go ahead with the Ottawa visit. Several months later she described her welcome.

> .... I felt there was something in the air. It was anything but comfortable. When I asked Miss Livingstone she said "she felt somewhat surprised that I should be sent down without the Minister previously notifying them of my visit." I said the minister has many responsibilities and doubtless the matter had escaped his memory and as I had been the representative for six years it seems scarcely necessary. [32]

Adelaide claimed that Bessie Livingstone was discourteous and antagonistic towards the Guelph school, and suspected one of the reasons for her opposition was jealousy. Miss Livingstone apparently wanted to be the final authority in the Ottawa area, Adelaide said, yet was unaware of the latest developments in domestic science as she "had been out of the country five years." [33]

On her part, Bessie Livingstone found Adelaide equally difficult to deal with. In late October 1902, Richard Harcourt informed Adelaide:

> I am in receipt of letters (very bellicose in nature) from Ottawa, concerning your recent visit there. You are evidently not persona grata to our Ottawa friends. I do not know what is to be done about it. I must take every step possible to hasten the installation of a suitable equipment. Have you seen the Renfrew equipment? Would it be suitable? [34]

Although Harcourt told her that the letters from Ottawa were confidential, Adelaide asked for more details.

> I would like to know what their grievance is? and feel sure that it would be better for me to know. If I have made a mistake, I should like to know as it might prevent a repetition, and if I am unjustly accused I must protect my position. So far as I know I have not done anything to cause such an attitude. I meet discourtesy with all the calmness possible, and do not think it fair that my efforts should be handicapped by some mischievous element of which I am unconscious. [35]

Along with the "mischievous elements", Adelaide was unconscious of her own shortcomings. Convinced as she was of her own expertise in domestic science, she rarely allowed for any opposing viewpoint. In the Ottawa case, the difficulties were increased by the fact that Miss Livingstone was British. While Adelaide had many British-born friends and acquaintances, she also harboured a certain resentment towards some women of that nationality who looked on "colonial" efforts in domestic science as inadequate. Her resentment was deepened by a belief, encouraged by conversations with British acquaintances, that many of the domestic science teachers who came to Canada from England (and less frequently from Scotland or other parts of the UK) were second rate: the top notch leaders had no difficulty in finding positions in their own country.

Nevertheless, despite the clash with Bessie Livingstone, Adelaide was able to overcome her personal feelings and fulfill Harcourt's request for advice on school equipment. She recommended that, since the Renfrew equipment was unsuitable for the Ottawa school, drawings of more suitable equipment should be made and submitted for Miss Livingstone's approval. It was gestures such as this which helped Adelaide maintain her many strong supporters. For example, after critical comments appeared in a Hamilton newspaper, an anonymous Hamiltonian wrote a letter attacking the board of Education for "trying to beat out Mrs. Hoodless by insinuating that as a government official her remarks should be discounted."[36] The writer ended by saying that if this "bright and brainy"[37] woman was a product of domestic science training, every community should spend money on that type of education. Seemingly, for every critic there was at least one fan willing to defend Adelaide and her beliefs. In the final analysis, it was probably Adelaide's charm that advanced the cause of domestic science as much as the worth of the subject itself. As one college president told her after hearing her speak:

> I would give a very liberal salary to any woman who would bring into my college the spirit which you have introduced into the education of women in regard to homemaking.[38]

Chapter Eleven

A Trip to England

Adelaide's life became positively hectic in 1899. As usual, she continued to bring pressure on the Hamilton Board of Education over the question of domestic science. In early February, she travelled to the United States, for inspection tours of domestic science programmes in Philadelphia and Washington. Her report, which she completed 10 March, was largely a repetition of her standard arguments for the introduction of domestic science training.

One noteworthy section of the report dealt with the basis for objections to domestic science:

> As the chief objections to the introduction of these subjects into the Public School System of Ontario are — 1st, overcrowded curriculum; 2nd, expense; it may be well to submit evidence concerning such important points. N. B. Powell, Superintendent of the Washington Schools says, in reference to the effect such instruction upon other studies: — "I feel very sure that the unbiassed testimony of all connected with the public schools of Washington is that our academic work has been substantially and perceptibly improved and made more agreeable to the pupils by virtue of the co-related manual of exercises. the result has been health-giving and has changed the attitude of children's minds toward the subject of education.
>
> Dr. McAlister, for many years superintendent of schools in Philadelphia, now President of the Drexel Institute, says: — "The thing which must be kept constantly in mind is that the new studies are not simply annexed to the existing curriculum, but are to be worked into it as an integral part of the general education given in the schools."
>
> ...An exaggerated idea is usually entertained concerning the expense of such instruction. There are two points of view from which it is well to consider this question. 1st. The relative value of these subjects as they affect the general principles of education; 2nd. The economic value of such instruction. The returns have been so sure and satisfactory in every case where such training has been provided, that the matter of expense has been of minor importance. No objections have been raised by ratepayers after a fair trial of the system. [1]

Based on domestic science courses in Halifax and Montreal, Adelaide estimated it would cost $200 to $300 to furnish a classroom for the subject, $500 to $600 for a teacher's annual salary, $100 for materials, and $100 for extras including fuel.

The report was a routine one, a result of Adelaide's association with the Ontario government. Less routine was a brief battle she waged in the

London Free Press .

It started on March 4th, when a teacher named S. Baker wrote a critical report on Adelaide's domestic science textbook, and his own treatment at a London Local Council of Women meeting.

> I was refused permission and the usual time to state my objections to the introduction of domestic science in our Public schools at the Local Council of Women, although invited to the meeting and the platform. Some of the ladies present were able to understand my objections if the president could not, and now think as I do. When adverse criticism of any important measure is prevented there is but one conclusion — it is feared. [2]

Baker argued that domestic science was "everything that relates to the home.... Domestic economy consists of the practice of the results on operations of the study of the science." [3] While he did not deny the value of domestic science, he questioned the feasibility of its introduction to public schools and attacked Adelaide's textbook for focusing almost exclusively on cooking "excepting an odd photograph." [4] The contents, he felt, were beyond the comprehension of the students they were meant for, especially the passages concerning food chemistry.

In Baker's opinion, students already had enough to learn and it was simply not sensible to introduce subjects such as those in Adelaide's text.

> In connection with my school, some fourteen years ago, I had my boys taught by a handy man the use of tools — the hammer, saw, chisel, plane, blacksmith's anvil and forge, and the girls were taught plain sewing and patching, knitting, and darning by the lady teachers. These subjects being manual, and the rudiments of the domestic art, not domestic science, were a rest from the other studies of school. The attempt to teach more is folly. [5]

He concluded by urging opposition to domestic science in London. Adelaide's response was fierce.

> I beg to say that were the writer of the letter and the text-book, which he devotes so much time to, the only consideration involved, I should let the matter pass with silent contempt. The criticism of the book is so puerile and so absolutely devoid of knowledge concerning the subject or of common fairness, that it is not worth noticing. But when misleading statements... which appear on the eve of an important action about to be taken by the & London Board of Education are made... then I feel justified in the interest of truth and justice to prove the untruthfulness of them. [6]

Adelaide cited various instances of the benefits derived from domestic science and the establishment of programmes in England, Belgium, Germany and the US. Mr. Baker ("it must be a man as no woman would be so illogical or unfair" [7]) wrote an additional letter, which appeared on 10 March this time, his attack was more personal.

Mrs. Hoodless' adjectives regarding myself are valueless. The people of Hamilton know her much better than I do, and think her opinion not worth much, as shown by their action on Domestic Science last year... invectives are no arguments, being simply the defence of a weak cause. The "lie that is a half truth" is not mine. When a lady uses this language a man scarcely knows what to do.[8]

Baker offered to make a five dollar bet with Adelaide to prove his point, a facetious suggestion which was never accepted, possibly because his letter included another attack on the "little red book." He had previously referred to another text being prepared by London Local Council president Mrs. Boomer, and apologized for the error when he found that this was not the case. "I know that she would write a much better than the authorized work."[9]

As a consequence of this newspaper feud and another adverse publicity, the London Board of Education refused to consider a request for the question of domestic science to be examined. Mrs. Boomer addressed the refusal in her own letter to the editor:

"A good cause is seldom won without a good fight," and one does not usually bring into use a gatling gun merely to kill a hedge sparrow, therefore those who opposed the introduction of domestic science into our schools must have considered it an antagonist to be reckoned with or they would not in their manifest desire to avoid a discussion have committed the indiscretion and have risked the inevitable comments upon their marked discourtesy to the large number of our leading citizens, men and women, who, personally and by petition, came before them on Tuesday night, by refusing to permit their request to be submitted to the Standing Committee, a course usually taken in the case of every matter, which, even in the smallest degree, affects the intersts of our schools.[10]

It was Adelaide who had the last word in this phase of the London domestic science battle, however. Her rebuttal to the last of Baker's letter was icy and terse:

I beg to say that, as the teaching of Domestic Science in the public schools is not a personal matter, I decline to discuss it as such.

When the Board of Education is prepared to give the question its serious and intelligent consideration and some actual benefit to the cause of practical education is likely to result the reform, then I shall be quite willing to prove the truthfulness of any statements for which I am responsible, if so desired. Under existing circumstances, it is not worth the trouble. It is time enough to discuss a text-book — which has been approved by noted authorities, who understand the subject— when its use is made obligatory.[11]

Meanwhile, Hamilton's Board of Education continued to resist efforts to introduce the new subject. In a letter dated 13 April, the Local Council of Women had asked the Board to reconsider. The Internal Management Committee refused. On 11 May, they recommended ''that no action be taken on the resolutions of the Local Council of Women re. the teaching of Domestic Science.''[12]

Despite these setbacks in Hamilton and London, Adelaide continued to gain support elsewhere. She had apparently written to Charles Tupper to enlist his support in persuading another, unnamed politician in the cause of domestic science. Tupper, the same man who had so vocally opposed the VON and the Aberdeens, replied courteously,

> I thank you very much for your letter of the 7th inst. and enclosure. I may say in the outset I will be very glad to do anything in my power to further the very important work in which you take so deep an interest — technical education in Canada. I cannot approach the gentleman you name at the present time because I am pressing him for support that is absolutely necessary in another direction, but at the proper time I will not hesitate to put before him in the best manner I can the admirable suggestion you have made. I think it is quite possible that the Government may be induced to aid in this important work and I shall not fail to bring it before the notice of Parliament when a suitable opportunity offers.[13]

Whatever disappointment Adelaide felt at this reply was quickly dissipated as she prepared to leave for England. The International Council of Women was having its first conference since Chicago, and Adelaide was looking forward to the trip. Not only was she an official delegate of considerable stature, she had also been commissioned to report on her trip for readers of the Toronto *Mail and Empire.*

The reports, which cover roughly a month from late June to early July, offer a rare glimpse into Adelaide's personality. Although many of her writings survive, they are almost exclusively reports, correspondence with officials,, and letters to the editor, generally very formal, and, at times, tedious. In her desire to further the cause of domestic science, Adelaide often repeated herself; often it becomes difficult to distinguish one article or speech from another.

The reports from England were of an entirely different nature. In effect, they are like long letters home, gossipy, full of little details about who and what she saw, and her impressions. Some of the subject matter is serious, some related directly to domestic science, but a great deal of it is quite lively and entertaining. Adelaide manages to communicate a great deal of the excitement and enthusiasm she was obviously experiencing.

The Atlantic crossing took eight days, with weather so wet and miserable that everyone was depressed. Adelaide's spirits lifted when she reached Liverpool, partly because of the efficient handling of travel arrangements, partly because of a visit to the Liverpool Technical College. Here she was on familiar ground, and thoroughly impressed with what she saw.

I only wish it were possible for me to convey some idea of the wonderful work done through the agency of this college. The committee of the Liverpool Training school has arranged lessons in cookery for almost every conceivable class of women and girls, in every variety of school and institution, and always with the same satisfactory results.[14]

Upon reaching London, Adelaide's schedule became unbelievably crowded. All kinds of social functions had been arranged to coincide with the International Congress. The women attending came from more than twenty countries, including New Zealand, Argentina, and Iceland, and from all levels of society. To satisfy her readers' interest in the British aristocracy, Adelaide listed some of the high born women she encountered, including the Duchesses of Portland, Westminster, Marlborough, and Sutherland, and Lady Dudley, Lady Grandy, and Lady Dufferin. She also attempted to change some stereotypical ideas about the women of upper class British society.

We were much impressed with the youthful appearance of the majority of the ladies of high degree. It seemed to be pretty generally understood on our side of the water that a duchess should be at least middle-aged and the personification of grace and dignity. That the latter qualifications are thoroughly developed is very apparent, but in appearance they are anything but awe inspiring.[15]

She told of her visit to the Charing Cross bazaar:

The charming, unaffected manners of the ladies in charge of the stalls were one of the most delightful features of the occasion. When by some chance word they found we were from Canada, they not only gave us much gratuitous information, but seemed thoroughly interested.[16]

As well as attending social events, many of the visitors wanted to see famous London landmarks. Among those on Adelaide's list was the famous market at Covent Garden, which she and her companions visited at five o'clock one morning.

The flowers were beyond description, vegetables of every sort in abundance, everything packed in baskets ready for handling. But, oh, the fruit! Small baskets of cherries containing from four to six quarts, for 30 shillings ($7.50), five pounds of strawberries for 3 shillings, peaches 8 pence each; other fruit equally expensive. What kindly remembrances of Grimsby peaches and other luxuries, within reach of the most limited income, are aroused under such conditions. [17]

No matter where she was, Adelaide was always the practical housewife, ever conscious of food prices. Her London experiences increased her appreciation of the bountiful harvest of fruit grown in the Niagara Penninsula near Hamilton.

The first meeting of the Congress of Women took place on the afternoon of 26 June in the Convocation Hall of Church House, Westminster. Most of the representatives appeared in modern dress, although a few wore native costumes. One of the most celebrated participants was eighty-year-old Susan B. Anthony, who reminisced on sixty years of feminist reform.

Adelaide was impressed by "the intense earnestness and wide range of thought" displayed by the speakers.

> To those who anticipate the demoralization of the home life in what is popularly called the "emancipation of woman," the words of the president may prove comforting. On summing up the aims of the council, among other things, she said: — "Woman's first mission must be her home, and by it she would ever be judged. The dream of all was a better country, which meant, in other words, a land of better, happier, truer and holier homes." The increased educational advantages and wider outlook has aroused a much higher conception of women's responsibility in regard to the influence of the home as a factor in a nation's welfare. This was very apparent in all the discussions to-day.[18]

The Congress was scheduled to run eight days, and was divided into four sections: Educational, which included child life and training; School, encompassing literary, scientific, manual and physical training, as well as post-secondary education; the professions; and the legislative and industrial section. Already Adelaide admitted, the number of activities was taking its toll. "It reminds one of the World's Fair, where the exhibits were so numerous and beautiful that the visitor got bewildered. Here one gets mentally confused."[19] And, if the mental confusion generated by speeches and discussion were not enough, the social events took up a great deal of time as well. The first major event took place following the opening of the congress. It was held at Stafford House, home of the Duchess of Sutherland. Adelaide was overawed by the beauty of the mansion, the flowers decorating the halls and reception rooms, the Hungarian band in native costume, and the picture gallery, which included work by Murillo, Titian, and Van Dyck. "Only generations could produce such a magnificent result in general perfection of detail as is displayed in Stafford house."[20]

It soom became apparent that several members of British society intended to vie with one another in impressing delegates to the Congress. "We are to have other social priviledges extended," Adelaide told her readers...

> among the most interesting being the garden party given by Lady Rothschild and Mrs. Leopold de Rothchild on July 4th and the reception given by the Countess Warwick on the 5th. Lord Strathcona gives a reception to Canadians to celebrate Dominion day, on the evening of June 30th, and Lady Aberdeen gives a farewell on the 6th. These are only a few of the kindnesses extended to the visitors. We are tired now, what we shall be in another week is "another story."[21]

What the next week brought was more of the same: discussions at the Congress, and lavish entertainments in the evenings and on weekends.

The study at Eastcourt

For many of the women, one of the high points occurred on 8 July, when they encountered Queen Victoria. A tea was served at St. George banquet hall, and beforehand the 250 delegates assembled in the quadrangle at Windsor Castle.

> As there were too many to receive individual notice, it was arranged...
> Her Majesty would drive slowly along the line as she passed out for her
> afternoon drive.[22]

The carriage stopped beside Lady Aberdeen, to whom the Queen spoke for a few moments. Nearby was Mrs. Sanford of Hamilton.

> She also received a cordial handclasp. After this Her Majesty drove very
> slowly along the line, bowing most graciously as she passed the
> representatives from India, who, in their picturesque native costumes,
> proved very attractive. Her Majesty looked the picture of health and
> every inch a queen. The Princess Beatrice and some other members
> of the Royal family were with the Queen, but no one looked at them, all
> eyes and heads were on the sweet, womanly face, who had paid such a
> marked compliment to the Woman's Congress, and to our own beloved
> president. After the Royal carriage passed the party we were enter-
> tained at tea and shown through the castle, returning to town by the
> special 7 o'clock, a delightful and happy party.[23]

In between attendance at such social events and sessions of the Congress, Adelaide found time to visit technical schools in London, a privilege which had been arranged through the Ontario Department of Education. Her visits, and the reports she heard at the Congress, led her to conclude

> that Canada is behind the times in its reception of this idea has been
> made very clear. That she is 25 years behind the times in practical
> education is still more apparent. But listening as I did, very attentively
> to the various discussions, I arrived at a very positive conclusion, and
> that was that our delay has not been an unmixed misfortune. The efforts
> along these lines have been largely experimental, and in many cases the
> structure has been torn down and rebuilt. Therefore, I believe, that as
> Canada cannot afford expensive educational experiments, it is a better
> position to build well and safely, when the benefits of these experiments
> may be obtained; and as it is easier to build on experience, even if that
> of other countries, we may hope to provide for the new country
> something infinitely superior to the efforts which have been handicapped
> in the older countries by traditional customs and laws.[24]

She was adamant on the latter point, feeling it would never do to adopt the British system of domestic science education wholesale.

> ...we shall have to work out our own system. The conditions in London
> are so peculiar, traditional customs, laws and regulations are so
> intertwined, it is a veritable puzzle, and most difficult to understand the
> meaning of various guilds, country councils, city council, and other

bodies which control this vast populace. We have much to be thankful for in Canada. It is very nice to have a history, but like many other blessings, it has its drawbacks.[25]

Almost immediately after the Congress, Adelaide attended the first British Poultry Conference at Reading College, where she had been invited to give an address

What a comfort it was to know that I had at least a dozen hens at home which enabled me to qualify for the position. Well, as I had just graduated from a woman's congress it seemed quite the proper thing to take a post-graduate course at a man's conference, and I felt somewhat important over being the only Congress woman invited to take part in the proceedings.[26]

She did not report in detail on her address, except to say

I mentioned the noticeable absence of Canadian food products (except cheese) among the announcements on the "boards" at the different markets, and said it made a Canadian feel rather overshadowed in the affections of the Mother Country by foreign nations. This brought out many ideas on the subject, which convinced me beyond question that if our people would ship their goods in a more scientific manner they would be well received.[27]

She did, however, compare the Congress of Women and the male-dominated Poultry Conference, preferring the latter since only one paper was read each session, allowing ample time for discussion. But she added, "in justice to the Woman's Congress I must say that as speakers, in comparison, the men were rather at a discount, but they take such a thoroughly utilitarian view of everything."[28]

In her newspaper report on the conference, she also added some sharp observations about the British people she encountered.

I looked around the room in order to form some idea of the English farmer, and concluded that they were a remarkably well-dressed, well-educated sample of mankind, and at once decided to make my boy an English farmer. But later I found that they were nearly all gentlemen of leisure, or landed magnates, who, for the good of humanity, had turned their attention to poultry farming. As the English people must have "chicken", it must be of the best quality, and they were experimenting so as to secure this desirable end. Several ladies (some with titles) were among the most interested numbers.[29]

If the differences between Canadian and English chicken farmers were glaringly obvious, the differences between politicians on either side of the ocean were not. Adelaide had certainly had plenty of experience with the Canadian variety, and reached the conclusion that the English were not so very different.

... the conference was opened by a very handsome, well-dressed, stereotypical Englishman, with the usual elegant platitudes, which I find quite as common to the English politician as to the Canadian, saying a great deal without a point, which, I suppose is the perfection of political tact.... He made everyone happy, and got away before the real business began, so that he should not be inveigled into any promises of Government support, etc., in a word, fulfilled his mission in a very creditable manner.[30]

If her comments were somewhat acidic, it can only be attributed to Adelaide's exhaustion. She seems to have become a little homesick by this time, and increasingly disillusioned with the perfect manners she encountered everywhere.

Another strong impression has been given me concerning the social life, and we have seen a good deal— the "one pattern" man and woman which prevails. The society manner is so thoroughly cultivated, one almost knows beforehand what the next person one meets will say and do. There is a marked absence [sic] of the striking individuality one meets in America, where it is certainly impossible to imagine what the next person will say or do. It gets a little "heavy", and one sometimes feels like "breaking out," just to see how they will take it. But beneath and beyond it all there is an individuality which in high life is not always what it should be, but which is very delightful. The culture and comfort of a well-ordered English home is beyond criticism. The gentle courtesies which are always unobtrusively paid to strangers, the generous hospitality, the desire to make one like England, and the self-satisfied, comfortable belief that you can't help liking it, all got to complete the charm.[31]

Despite the diplomatic references to English hospitality, exhaustion was making Adelaide querulous. "Why is it my fate to strike discussions on food and kindred subjects?"[32] she asked after a visit to the House of Commons in which the subject of debate was food adulteration.

> I have not been able to get away from it for two successive days since I came to London. It must be the popular question. Well, I heard more about oleomargarine and butter, strawberry ices, and sundry articles of diet this afternoon than I have ever heard before. To be candid, there was an immense amount of "twaddle" talked, and I came to the conclusion that after all there were some things in legislation upon which women could give a few pointers.[33]

In spite of the link between the subject of the debate and her own interests, Adelaide was irritated.

> Why will English people speak so indistinctly? It was almost impossible to follow the discussion, and I confess it was a great relief when a thoughtful member offered to take us to tea on the terrace.[34]

By August, Adelaide was home again, and likely used the rest of the summer to recuperate from her English visit. If she did, it was time well spent, for, with the arrival of autumn, she was once again plunged into a whirlwind of activities and controversy.

Chapter Twelve

A School for Domestic Science Teachers

Some time after her return from England, Adelaide travelled to Philadelphia to inspect schools there for the Department of Education. During her visit, she was interviewed, and her comments appeared under the heading "The Good Canadian Hubby." After describing Adelaide as "a beautiful woman, and calls herself with pride, a domestic woman,"[1] the article quoted her as saying

> In Canada, women have not the provocation for suffrage agitation that the women in the U.S. have. In Canada, as soon as the men are convinced of the necessity of women's help in municipal affairs, they give the women by invitation what they want.[2]

What Adelaide did not add was that it was not often easy to convince men on various subjects, including that of domestic science education. Nor were women much easier to convince. Toward the end of the year, Adelaide felt compelled to write a letter to a Hamilton newspaper, chastizing Hamiltonians for the lack of support for the soon-to-be opened Normal School of Domestic Science and Art.

It had been hoped that the citizens of Hamilton could be persuaded to support the school. The Ontario government had offered $1,500 yearly towards operating costs, but there were many other expenses to be met. Adelaide explained,

> Every effort has been made to provide a building in keeping with such a progressive movement. Yet not one citizen has shown sufficient public spirit to come forward and offer one thousand dollars to help establish the first training school for teachers (without which nothing can be done) of technical subjects.... The committee in charge of the proposed training school has, after a long struggle and encouraged by the generous sympathy of the Hon. G.W. Ross, determined to make a last effort to establish the school without a new building. Therefore alterations are being made to the old YWCA building, and arrangements about completed for the opening in January.[3]

Although, as she pointed out, this was not strictly a local matter, since the teachers who graduated from the school would find jobs throughout the province, and possibly across the country, Adelaide and the committee were hopeful that some citizens or citizens of the "ambitious city" would see fit to contribute the needed money.

To her disappointment, Adelaide had little success in overcoming public apathy to the project. Her efforts were further hindered when it was announced that the principal of the school would be Miss A. G. E. Hope, who had run domestic science programmes in Boston schools for fifteen years. Immediately, Adelaide and the committee were criticized for hiring a Yankee rather than a Canadian.

Initially, she chose to ignore the criticisms which appeared in the Hamilton papers, feeling that "the facts were so well known here it was not considered worth refuting."[4] But when similar criticisms appeared in a Toronto newspaper, Adelaide decided to reply. She firmly denied the charge of "disloyalty to Canadian teachers," explaining

> Being a normal school for training teachers of domestic science for Public Schools, it was necessary to secure instructors, who, by experience and wide knowledge, could introduce the latest and improved methods. As a pioneer in this work in Canada... I have reason to know that Canadian teachers have absolutely no knowledge of Public school methods of teaching domestic science, as they have had no opportunity for acquiring such knowledge....
>
> It was opposition to bringing alien teachers into Canada that led us to persevere in arousing our educational authorities to their responsibility and to secure a suitable building and staff of experienced teachers which would enable Canadian girls to compete with those from any other country.[5]

She concluded by pointing out that Miss Hope was not American but British

> The only alien on the staff is the director of the domestic science art department, who is a graduate of the celebrated Pratt Institute, Brooklyn, no Canadian with the requisite training being available for this department.[6]

Regardless of the criticism, the Ontario Normal School of Domestic Science and Art opened only a month later than planned, on 1 February 1900. As the first school for teachers of domestic science and art in the country, it received full coverage from all three Hamilton newspapers.

At seven o'clock in the evening, various dignitaries, the organizing committee, their families, and interested citizens gathered at the renovated YWCA building on Main Street. Among the guests were George Ross, now premier of Ontario, Bishop DuMoulin of Niagara, Hamilton mayor J. V. Teetzel, and Professor Tracey of the University of Toronto.

The YWCA building had undergone major improvements at a cost of $4,500. On the main floor was a large reading room and a reception room. The second floor consisted of two classrooms, matrons' rooms and lavatories, while two more classrooms took up the third floor. In these, skylights augmented the new electrical lighting which had been installed. The basement contained another reading room and a dining room which would do double duty as a gymnasium until further renovations could be carried out. Anticipating the need for more space, Adelaide and her committee were hoping to add another building containing a gymnasium, classrooms, and dormitories.

> The interior woodwork throughout is of pine, and everything is of the most serviceable nature. The principal colors used in the decoration are red, with trimmings of stone color. The place is heated with hot water.... [7]

Once the throngs of visitors had inspected the premises, Bishop DuMoulin read a prayer and Premier Ross officially declared the building open. The group then walked to the nearby Centenary Church lecture room for an evening of congratulatory speeches.

For Adelaide, it was a night of unsurpassed triumph. In his opening remarks, Mayor Teetzel gave full credit for the completion of the project to Adelaide and her associates, and his remarks drew loud applause. George Ross, too, credited Adelaide with making the normal school a reality. "For her persistence and for unswerving determination to accomplish her aim and purpose he believed Mrs. Hoodless to be the peer of almost any woman he had ever met." [8] Several times throughout the course of the evening the speakers' praise of Adelaide provoked appreciative responses from the audience. And, when Adelaide herself was introduced as the "mother" of the school and stood to speak, the clapping reached deafening proportions.

Basking in the approval of the audience and the warm glow brought by the success of one of her fondest dreams, Adelaide read congratulatory letters from Lady Minto, the president of the WCTU, Sir Wilfred Laurier, Sir Charles Tupper, and Senator George Cox. She spoke briefly, thanking those who had helped her, especially her family and George Ross, and requesting donations of "pictures, china, books, table linen, cutlery and equipment for the gymnasium." [9] She also expressed her pride in the work she and her committee had accomplished, concluding with a remark directed to Mayor Teetzel. "After ten years service, Mr. Mayor, I present to you, on behalf of the city, my contribution. I can't give money. I give my services." [10] Adelaide returned to her seat with the sound of more applause ringing in her ears.

If there was one dark cloud in evidence that night, it appeared in the reference made by George Ross to continued public resistance to domestic science.

> For the last six or seven years he had been endeavouring to cultivate a public opinion in favour of domestic science, and up to this minute, he was bound to say, his efforts in that respect had not been very successful. It seemed to take a long time to create and build up public opinion for some of these changes. [11]

Cooking class, Hamilton ca. 1902.

Yet, even as he made the statement, Ross demonstrated optimism. He told how, after Adeliade's visits to various towns throughout the province, she invariably reported that what people wanted were teachers to set up domestic science programmes. In opening a school to train such teachers, Ross hoped he was paving the way for increased support of the programme throughout the province.

When the festivities were over, the real work began. Adelaide, as president of the school, was in charge of overall management. Her staff was highly qualified. In addition to Miss Hope and Mrs. Ward, the "alien" director of the domestic art department, it included Miss Norris, principal of the School of Household Science in Toronto, who would teach food chemistry and bacteriology, and Miss E. Howell, a certified physical education specialist. Many of the lectures would be handled by professionals from other institutions who were experts in their fields, such as J. A. McLellan, M.A., LL.D., principal of the Ontario Normal College, who would teach psychology and the history of education, and Doctors L. W. Cockburn and Mabel Henderson, who would lecture on the handling of emergencies. At the opening of the school, seven women, all graduates of normnal schools or universities, were enrolled. By the end of the year, enrollment would climb to eighteen.

One of Adelaide's duties as president was to publicize the school and its aims, both through speeches and articles. One of the most comprehensive descriptions of the school appeared in a special Christmas issue of the *Spectator* that year.

> The aim of the Ontario Normal School of Domestic Science and Art is the one laid down by Ruskin: "First, feed people; second, dress them; third, lodge them, and last, please with arts or other subjects of thought." In order to develop this important phase of education it is necessary to have trained teachers with this object in view.
>
> The following course of study has been arranged for those entering the Normal class: Psychology and history of education, physics, chemistry, bacteriology, hygiene, household economy, dietics, food economics, cookery, invalid cookery, marketing, home nursing and emergencies, laundry work and physical culture. In Domestic Art the course of study is as follows: First year—Psychology, hygiene, physical culture, business methods, practice teaching, sewing, millinery, dressmaking, drawing— color and form. Second year— History of education, normal methods, practice teaching, physical culture, sewing, millinery, dressmaking, costume design.
>
> Technical or special classes in domestic science are offered to young women who may desire to qualify for the every day duties of the home, or who may wish to become experts in special subjects. Instruction is given in plain, high-class and chafing dish cookery, invalid and nurse's class, dietaries, marketing and laundry work. The work of the school is prosecuted upon several lines with four distinct aims in view:

1. Education pure and simple; the purpose being the harmonious development of the faculties.

2. Normal: the preparation of the student to become a teacher. Normal training is at present given in the Department of Domestic Science and in the Department of Domestic Art.

3. Supplementary and special: intended for the benefit of those who wish to add to the training of school or college by attention to special subjects conducing to more intelligent direction of domestic, social, or philanthropical interests.[12]

In her determination to promote the Hamilton school, Adelaide sometimes made enemies of her colleagues in the domestic science field. For instance, at the eighth annual convention of the National Household Economic Association in Toronto, she was asked what she saw as the major obstacles to the implementation of domestic science programmes. Adelaide's response was unequivocal:

Incompetent and injudicious teachers. A great mistake can be made, and has been, in some places, of putting untrained, unprepared and incompetent teachers in charge of cooking schools, and calling that domestic science.[13]

Such remarks were hardly designed to endear her to many teachers. Adelaide frequently criticized women, who, having acquired the skills, opened cooking schools and referred to themselves as domestic science teachers. Paradoxically, she considered herself qualified to teach domestic science classes, although she had no formal training, and, in fact, would be considered unqualified by the most highly educated domestic science experts. Adelaide's blindness in this area is especially ironic in view of her comments at the National Household Economic Association convention. "Now it is 'my way,' and 'your way,' and the 'other way,' and 'any way,' instead of 'the way,' the only right way of doing housework."[14]

This, of course, was the source of major divisions within the domestic science crusade. Adelaide referred to the problem on several occasions, for it was impossible to ignore. Because the field of domestic science was relatively new, and because methods and schools had sprung up independently in several areas, there was no consensus regarding methods, which is perhaps understandable. It seems incredible that no one explored the premise that housekeeping, cooking, and other domestic work could not be handled in the same way as, for example, laboratory procedures. Lab conditions and equipment were far more standardized than the conditions prevailing in homes. Each home and each family is unique, yet it never seems to have occurred to Adelaide and her colleagues that allowances had to be made for this uniqueness, and the fact that many women did not have access to well-equipped modern kitchens anywhere but in domestic science schools. Consequently, workers in the field of domestic science reform were continually bickering over conflicting procedures and ideologies, to the detriment of the movement as a whole.

Adelaide ignored the bickering and continued her single-minded campaign to make her vision of domestic science education a reality. In addition to promoting the Normal School, she continually urged local school boards to introduce domestic science. She was especially active in Hamilton. On 9 March 1901, for example, she persuaded the Board of Education to allow two classes, consisting of 25 girls each, to attend domestic science courses at the Normal School. By the end of the school year, she was suggesting the Board take over the YWCA's Stuart Street building and use it as a centre for teaching domestic science. Initially, the special committee formed to look into the proposal rejected the idea. However, S. F. Lazier argued for acceptance as long as operating costs stayed below $300 annually. Lazier's recommendation was approved by a vote of six to five.

Presumably, the presence of the country's first training school for domestic science teachers was having its effect. Because of the school, Hamilton was gaining a reputation for progressiveness in education. Consequently, the Board of Education could hardly be seen as opposing progress. It was still political to consider costs before establishing new programmes, nevertheless, and to move slowly before making costly commitments. Despite deeply entrenched opposition from some of the school trustees, there were definite signs that the Board's attitude towards domestic science was softening, although Adelaide was continually disappointed with the apathy shown toward the school by local officials.

At the same time, she was afraid to relinquish control. When she learned a school of manual training was to be established in Hamilton and controlled by the Board of Education, she worried that this might eventually lead to the Board of Education's control of domestic science classes. She expressed her concerns in a letter to the Minister of Education, Richard Harcourt:

> I shall not hand it over yet. School boards are not reliable enough, made up as they are of all sorts & conditions of men.... It is woman's work & must have women associated with its development.[15]

Consequently, she aimed at having public school students taught domestic science under the aegis of the Normal School. By 16 December, she was able to celebrate a partial victory. Although the Board of Education chairman claimed "the whole scheme was the greatest fad ever brought before the Board and it would be a good job for Hamilton if Toronto got the school"[16] a recommendation was made that seventy-five pupils be taught domestic sciences at the Normal School, with "the distinct understanding that it is not to be taken as a permanent arrangement."[17] The Board also stipulated that the written consent of parents was required before students attended domestic science classes.

Lacking the gift of clairvoyance, Adelaide did not know that her long battle with the local school board was almost over. By the next October, Richard

Harcourt had notified the Hamilton Board of Education that domestic science was about to become a regular part of the curriculum in Ontario schools. As a result, the Board recommended the establishment of regular domestic science classes at the Caroline Street and King Edward schools.

There was a last ditch attempt to rouse public opinion against domestic science classes. The *Spectator* printed a critical piece, which Adelaide claimed, in a letter to the editor, was full of errors. Chief among these was the continual reference to ''cookery'' as synonymous with domestic science. Again the argument had been made that girls could be taught cooking and sewing at home. Adelaide retorted, ''Many women in Hamilton could teach their children to read and write, but they don't.''[18] This time, Adelaide's voice carried above the opposition's, and domestic science became an integral part of Ontario's educational system.

Chapter Thirteen

An Ambitious Project

Adelaide's plans for domestic science education were all-encompassing. Public school courses were only part of her scheme. Even as the Ontario Normal School of Domestic Science and Art opened, she and her committee were planning on its expansion. To this end, and to finance operating costs, Adelaide was actively seeking support for the institution. One of the more prominent patrons of the school was Donald Smith, Lord Strathcona, who wrote, "I know that in your hands it is capable of doing, and will do, good work in that very necessary branch of instruction."[1]

Yet, as Adelaide sought support for the school's present and future needs, and battled with apathy and disappointment, she was also working on a more ambitious project, the development of university courses in domestic science. It is difficult to determine where the idea originated. According to the Hoodless family tradition, Adelaide took credit for the idea, which, she said, was inspired during a visit to Bernard, who was a student at the Ontario Agricultural College in Guelph. But a letter from James Mills, OAC principal, dated 9 March 1900, suggests a different reality:

> I quite agree with you that it will be necessary for us to continue our agitation if we are to succeed in getting a Department of Domestic Science at the College. I think there is no place else where we can do such good work as such small outlay, because we have already the laboratories and appliances for instruction in horticulture, dairying, poultry, and the various sciences in their application to cooking and other arts. Hence I am glad to know that you are favourable to the establishment of such a Department in connection with the College, and shall be glad of any assistance which you may render in this direction.[2]

Mills' letter suggests the idea of a college course in domestic science originated with himself, or with someone affiliated with either the College or the Department of Agriculture, and that Adelaide was chosen as a likely organizer because of her success in promoting domestic science in public schools. Whatever the source of the idea, Adelaide soon made the cause her own.

Initially, efforts to establish a college course in domestic science had to take a back seat while Adelaide worked on other issues, including the crucial first year of the Normal School's operation. Eventually, though, she came to the conclusion that she would have to find a wealthy patron to help finance the project. Lord Strathcona was not a good choice, since he had already donated generously to the Normal School. But another candidate

Portrait of Sir William Christopher Macdonald by J. W. L. Forster.

came to mind one morning as she was brushing her teeth, according to her daughter Edna. He was Sir William Christopher Macdonald, who was already a patron of the National Council of Women, as well as an advocate of manual training for boys.

William Christopher Macdonald was born in Prince Edward Island in 1831, son of the president of the Island's legislative council. Although he despised smoking, at twenty-seven he established his own tobacco company, and eventually made a fortune.

Frugality was deeply ingrained in the new millionaire. A bachelor, he slept in an iron bed in a small room in his Montreal mansion. He saved string and wrapping paper, and wore his clothes until they were practically falling apart from age. While he had little formal education, he donated $11 million to McGill University, helping to make it one of the best centres of learning on the continent.

He also had an unpredictable streak, something Adelaide was likely aware of. At one point, Dr. Robert McKenzie, a sculptor and noted physical educationist, had requested a raise of $1,000. Without it, he would leave for the University of Pennsylvania. Regardless of the prestige McKenzie brought to McGill, Macdonald would not budge. "Professors will be giving dinner parties if they get such high salaries,"[3] he reputedly said.

Macdonald was not as hard as he appeared, however. McGill professor Henry "Marsh" Tory said after an interview, "Under a cold exterior," Macdonald was "warm hearted and possessed of great goodwill."[4] Perhaps Adelaide shared Tory's sentiments, but she undoubtedly realized that Macdonald might also be difficult to reach. His secretary, Mr. Stewart, jealously protected him from intruders. Moreover, there was an additional obstacle, although it is possible Adelaide was not aware of it. In April 1900, Lady Minto had written to Macdonald asking for financial support for an Ottawa school of domestic science. He refused to assist in

> this vague scheme, of which I have no proper measure, no idea where it begins, where it ends, or of what it specifically consists, and am therefore quite incompetent to discuss the subject intelligently.[5]

He ended by telling the Governor-General's wife that, even if he had more information on the project, he was already financially committed for the remainder of the year.

But nothing could divert Adelaide once her mind was made up, not even knowledge of an earlier refusal. Early in 1901, she met with Macdonald, and ascertained the likelihood of his support for the Guelph project. On 8 March, she wrote to him:

> Having occasion to visit O.A. College at Guelph last Tuesday, where my son is a very happy student, I discussed the question of establishing a training department for teachers, who could, through the co-operation of County Councils, Farmers and Women's Institutes, give scientific practical instruction to the inhabitants of rural districts without the

necessity of leaving home and acquiring a taste for the city life, etc.[6]

Emphasizing that Dr. Mills approved the plan, she discussed the possibility of amalgamating the Normal School with the proposed department, a move which Richard Harcourt supported. Apparently, the plan was to close the Normal School in Hamilton that June, then re-open in Guelph. But a new building would be needed if the plan was to become a reality, and a new building would cost money. There was little chance the government could offer the funds, since they had just financed a biology building at Guelph, hence Adelaide was asking for Sir William's support. By way of encouragement, she told him

> Mr. Harcourt assured me he thought there would be no difficulty in arranging for its maintenance. Indeed, I should be willing to undertake a campaign for an endowment, if the ball could only be set rolling. Education has been provided for everything in this country save the Industrial Arts, Agriculture and Domestic Economy. I send you a clipping from Saturday night's paper, showing what we have done already in spite of difficulties. What could we not do properly established? There are thirty-five Women's Institutes throughout Ontario, established in the village for farmers' wives and daughters. It was my privilege to organize the first one four years ago. The object is to improve social conditions in the country, to learn the best methods of butter making, poultry raising, fertilizing for gardens and flowers, how to treat insect pests, Sanitation, cookery, food values and how to keep the boys and girls in the rural homes.
>
> These Institutes have been intensely popular, but now they have got beyond the stage of discussion and are clamoring for teachers. Two of our students went to O.A.C. and took the dairy course and are now travelling teachers, but what are two, where hundreds could be employed?
>
> I was so impressed with the view you expressed and being so deeply interested on the same lines, I am anxious to draw your attention the opening ready, and the need of co-operation. I could work with redoubled zeal and enthusiasm if this ideal plan could be carried out.... Being a farmer's daughter I feel justified in making an appeal for their support, and my heart goes out to this plan as it never has to anything before, and I assure you if I can do anything towards carrying this effort to a successful issue, my poor talents shall be given freely. I am so glad my son has chosen Agriculture as a profession. I hope he may be of service to his country.[7]

Sir William's immediate response is unknown, although ultimately Adelaide's faith in his support proved well founded. Later that year, on a promotional trip to Eastern Ontario, she asked Richard Harcourt for permission to make a side trip to Montreal, to discuss the matter of a larger normal school with Sir William. Her letter to Harcourt tells of her discouragement with the situation in Hamilton, and her feeling that, if a board of directors or the government were more directly responsible for the school's operation she could do a better job fund raising. ''I can ask for money for the school with much better grace when it is not under my own direct control. It removes the personal aspect.''[8]

Yet, in spite of her reluctance to ask for funds, she was positively eager to visit Sir William. She told Harcourt that, a few years previously, Macdonald had assured Professor Robinson that, having financed manual training for boys he meant to do something for girls. Knowing this, Adelaide felt that she could definitely convince Macdonald to offer his financial support. She would be in Lindsay on Monday, 21 October, and Tuesday, 22 October, and could take the train to Montreal Tuesday night, before proceeding to Renfrew for the 24th and 25th. In Montreal, she would speak to Macdonald

> … simply as a personal matter.… I am willing to give my time if you will allow me travelling expenses. Sir Wm. & I are good friends & I have so much more faith in a personal interview. My plan is to get him to do for girls what he is doing for boys — only through the Department of Education.[9]

Harcourt granted permission, and, on Tuesday night Adelaide travelled to Montreal. After checking into the Windsor Hotel, she sent a note to Sir William asking him to visit her on his way to the office. He arrived around 9:30 a.m. Wednesday morning, and they were soon deeply engrossed in conversation.

It is likely that on this occasion — rather than at a two-hour luncheon they had shared several months earlier, as has been claimed — that Adelaide made heroic efforts to convince Macdonald to support domestic science. At one point he told her, ''I can't do this for Ontario unless I do something for Quebec.''

''Then build one in Quebec, too,'' Adelaide urged. ''They need it.''[10] Eventually, Macdonald College was established at Ste. Anne de Bellevue, west of Montreal.

Macdonald may not have made any definite commitments at that point, but he certainly was charmed by Adelaide's company and conversation. ''Upon arising to leave for his office [he] fairly gasped when he looked at his watch and found it was ten minutes to one.… I am very glad I came and believe something will come out of it.''[11]

Chapter Fourteen

More Victories

While Adelaide was hoping for progress with the Board of Education and the proposed domestic science college, she was also required to face some serious personal problems. John's business was failing. He had $42,000 in assets, but owed nearly $40,000, and so an assignee, C. J. Scott, was named to sell off his stock and equipment. It seems John's business problems had arisen more from misfortune than mismanagement, for a newspaper article wished him well, and speculated that when matters were settled he would open a new wholesale company. This eventually proved to be the case.

Although John and Adelaide had private assets with which to meet their living expenses, their financial condition was relatively uncertain for most of the year. These financial worries cast a pall over Adelaide's recent triumphs, and also necessitated her contributing to the household coffers, probably for the first time since her marriage. In the past, the money she had been paid as a representative of the Department of Education had been a welcome bonus. Now, the money was essential to maintain the Hoodless household, and Adelaide began to realize there wasn't quite enough of it.

Nevertheless, the beginning of 1902 did bring some satisfaction. On 2 January, Richard Harcourt wrote a congtatulatory letter. "You certainly must be credited with bringing into focus Sir William Macdonald's Ontario Education projects."[1]

Harcourt also promised to speak to the Premier and to Agricultural Minister Dryden about Adelaide's request to help draw up the curriculum for the new school at Guelph.

There was a second cause for triumph, too, when many of Adelaide's critics were defeated in local elections. "All of my supporters were elected,"[2] she told Harcourt gleefully on 8 January. Two days later, she was anxious again, asking to meet the minister in order to discuss a "serious matter."[3]

What the matter was became clear after Harcourt put off any meeting in the immediate future, due to his own pressing schedule. On 15 January, Adelaide wrote another letter, in which she expressed dissatisfaction with her ambiguous position with the Department of Education. She felt she could be more useful if she knew precisely where she stood, she told Harcourt, who, by this time, was aware of her financial difficulties.

> If my services ever were or ever will be of value, I must realize on them this year. It will take Mr. H. at least six months to get his affairs into an income producing shape. In the meantime my children's education —

& they are doing so well in their respective schools — depends on me. It would be very unfortunate for them to be removed at the close of the present term & unless I can get into harness and do my share I shall be obliged to make the change. You will therefore realize how anxious I am to work & get things definitely settled.[4]

By this time, only Bernard and Muriel were still in school. Edna was 19, and had "come out", for her name frequently appeared in the Hamilton society columns as a guest at various social functions. On many occasions, she was accompanied to teas and receptions and balls by her mother, less frequently by both parents. Like most of her contemporaries, Adelaide was doing what she could to ensure that her eldest daughter made a suitable marriage, although this additional responsibility must have taxed her energies when added to an already overpower workload.

There is a story from this period that Adelaide decided to cut down on household expenses by doing her own housework, with the help of her daughters, and so the housemaid was given notice. The girl was so devoted to the family— and Adelaide in particular— that she refused to leave, and offered instead to work without pay until the financial situation improved. If the story is true, it indicates how deeply attached to her many of Adelaide's acquaintants were.

Still, personal regard must be often sacrificed to political expediency. Harcourt's reply to Adelaide's request for a definite arrangement with the Department of Education was non-commital. Instead, he asked her to continue her missionary work, and Adelaide willingly accepted. One of the reasons she was happy to go was that her work now included organizing domestic science courses rather than just making speeches. While she was a competent and well-liked speaker, she was far more comfortable in taking action than in trying to persuade school boards and citizenry of the worth of domestic science courses.

In truth, Adelaide had extremely mixed feelings about her missionary work. She complained about the tribulations of a "travelling demonstrator"[5] including the hostility and ignorance she frequently encountered school boards. "I have not been associated with local school boards for three years without learning some of their peculiarities,"[6] she told Richard Harcourt. The best method of dealing with them, she confessed, was to create the impression that the idea of introducing domestic science courses was the Board's idea.

> It would be on the principle upon which a friend of mine says she manages her husband, "allows him to think he is having things his ways, while she is having her way all the time."[7]

Yet, while she could be flippant about her methods of handling boards, Adelaide was acutely aware of how vulnerable she was to criticism as both spokesmen for domestic science education in public schools and president

Left to right: Muriel Hoodless, Adelaide Hoodless, Edna Hoodless.

of a domestic science teacher's college. "Sometimes I have been afraid they thought I was activated by a desire to place my girls."[8]

It was typical of Adelaide that she would feel a close attachment to the young women who attended the Normal School, and who had become stalwart soldiers in her crusade. In fact, she often allowed personal feelings for many teachers to influence her judgement. After one trip, she told Harcourt, "The work in the London collegiate is very poor, but the teacher is so conscious of her deficiencies that one has not the heart to say anything."[9] Adelaide expected the situation would improve since the teacher planned to take specialized domestic science courses.

Between trips, Adelaide was still actively involved in the YWCA, although she had resigned from the executive of the National Council of Women in April 1901. Early in 1902, she published a financial statement on the YWCA domestic science classes, which had been taught through an arrangement with the Normal School. The agreement between the two organizations was due to end in June, and so the YWCA would once again have to bear the full expense of teaching young girls cooking and sewing, unless, of course, the Board of Education footed the bill. Adelaide used the report as an opportunity to criticize the lack of public support for domestic science:

> The Directors of the Y.W.C.A..... regret the removal of the Normal School and its strong financial support. Owing to so little encouragement being extended by the citizens of Hamilton, the responsibility has been very heavy, and it is believed that the interest of the Normal School will be advanced through its becoming an integral part of the Provincial system and under the direction of the Department of Education.[10]

Because of Adelaide's intimate connections with both the YWCA, its "technical institute", which provided domestic science instruction, and the Normal School, it is often difficult to determine where one organization ended and the other began, especially when relying on contemporary newspaper reports. What this financial statement revealed, however, was that the YWCA was more or less back to square one. The Association would have to finance and oversee the teaching of domestic science to girls, without assistance from the Normal School. Meanwhile, there was another problem to solve. Sir William Macdonald was quibbling about the arrangements at Guelph. He wanted assurances that the Ontario government would provide the property, and, as a result, George Ross wrote to him on 8 January, telling him that a site had been selected. Subsequent correspondence created more confusion, for on 13 February, Macdonald wrote to Professor Robertson

Dear Sir,

Your letter of 10th Feb. with inclosures received. Mr. Ross' letter reads thus "Allow me to say that the Government accepts with much appreciation a grant of $125,000 from Sir William Macdonald to be applied for the training of teachers in the elements of agriculture and of young women in domestic science on the terms set forth in the said memorandum."

The grant was not intended to be applied as above explicitly stated by the works which I have underlined. — There is a contradiction in the wording, because the terms set forth in the memorandum of 6th January stated that the $125,000 was for the erection of the buildings.

Mr. Ross is a very busy man and I have no doubt he means the terms to be as set forth in the memorandum, but as we are treating with a Government which is subject to change the wording of an agreement should be correct, so as to be free from misunderstanding by another Government.[11]

Eventually, the matter was cleared up to everyone's satisfaction, and on 7 March 1902 an Order in Council was issued:

...Sir William Macdonald, of Montreal, will donate the sum of one hundred and twenty five thousand dollars ($125,000) to provide for the province of Ontario, at the Ontario Agricultural College, at Guelph, (1) a building, including a Nature Study Plant-growing house and equipment, for the accomodation of teachers while taking short courses in Nature Study for rural schools, and class rooms, laboratories and other equipment necessary for courses of instruction and training in Domestic Economy or Household Science; and (2) a residence building to accomodate female students and teacher-students, daughters of farmers and others; on the conditions that the Government of the Province of Ontario (1) would approve in general of the proposals presented in a memorandum signed by James W. Robertson and dated Ottawa, January 6th, 1902, and (2) would agree, on behalf of the province of Ontario:- 1st, To provide instructors at the Ontario Agricultural College for short courses in Nature-Study for teachers from rural schools without charging any fee for a period of three years; 2nd, To provide a course or courses of instruction and training in Domestic Economy or Household Science of such a sort and under such conditions and regulations as the Government of the Province may see fit to make; and 3rd, To maintain for these purposes, such buildings and equipment as are mentioned under Parts 3 and 4 of the Memorandum."[12]

By this time, Adelaide had made a trip to Guelph to inspect the building site and to talk to Professor Robertson, as well as to visit her son Bernard. The elation she felt at the knowledge that her dream of advanced domestic science courses would soon become a reality was short-lived. By April, she was writing to Harcourt about a deficit at the Normal School. After reiterating all the work she had done in setting up the school and raising funds, she asked for government help in meeting the deficit. She also pointed out that, by laying the groundwork at the Hamilton school, she had virtually ensured the success of the Guelph project.

> The experimental stage has been covered to a great extent, and by the time the Macdonald Teachers College at Guelph is completed, the school will be in such concrete shape, that only better accomodations and enlarged facility will be required to place it on a level with the best training schools in America or elsewhere. [13]

Adelaide also emphasized that she would feel most uncomfortable in asking Hamiltonians for money to make up the deficit when it was well known that the Normal School would be leaving the city.

The government quietly absorbed the deficit, which pleased Adelaide, but she was soon miffed to learn that a Mrs. Joy had been hired to teach a proposed summer school of domestic science. Adelaide told Harcourt that, while Mrs. Joy was able to teach classes at the YWCA's technical school, in other words, to teach young girls, she was not qualified to teach domestic science to women who planned to teach the subject themselves. But it seems Mrs. Joy's qualifications were only a minor source of Adelaide's irritation: the real problem was that she felt she should have been consulted before the government hired anyone. As it turned out, the summer courses were not offered in 1902.

A letter written by James Mills, President of the Ontario Agricultural College, also helped smooth Adelaide's ruffled feathers. In it, he told her,

> I shall be glad to have you outline courses of study such as you suggested in your former letter. I do not yet know what others may have to say in the matter, especially Professor Robertson; but I shall be glad to have your best suggestions, presented in systematic form, that we may talk them over together and reach a conclusion.... [14]

Mill's respect for Adelaide's expertise in domestic science was enhanced by a cordial personal relationship, for Edna Hoodless was a guest of his daughters on at least one occasion, and Adelaide undoubtedly enjoyed the family's hospitality on her frequesnt visits to Guelph.

In spite of her cordial relationship with Mills, Adelaide was going through a difficult period. Whether it was her family's financial crisis, her amibiguous position with the Department of Education, or the onset of menopause, (she was 45), Adelaide had more than the usual number of emotional ups and downs during 1902 and 1903. Her letters to Harcourt often take a whining tone. ''I wish I could have more definite work for the next month or two, as I am very anxious to make some money,''[15] she wrote to Harcourt in early May. Shortly afterwards, she visited the School of Education in Chicago, where she caught a bad cold. Unlike her first trip to the city during the Columbian Exposition, this trip to the "windy city" was disheartening. "It is a horrible place. Dante must have had Chicago in mind!"[16] Nor was she terribly impressed by the school's methods. "I find we are quite up to date in our methods at the school here."[17]

That view was further vindicated by June, when the results of the final examinations of the Normal School were published. Six students had graduated as teachers of domestic science and arts, and one, Mary McPherson, had won the Minto Gold Medal for Domestic Science, an award sponsored by the Governor-General's wife. It was another feather in Adelaide's cap, although it did not help her forget her money problems.

Adelaide's worries about money were justified. If cash was in short supply, she needed to be paid as quickly as possible to avoid going into debt. The government was not always prompt in reimbursing her for trips she took on its behalf. On June 25th, for instance, she was complaining to Harcourt, reminding him that she had not been reimbursed for Chicago. Adelaide was particularly anxious at this time because she was facing the added expense of a trip to Saint John and the National Council convention, which started on July 4th.

In addition to social activities, which included a picnic at Manchester Beach and parties in the members' homes, the Council handled a good deal of business at the Saint John convention. As usual, Adelaide publicized domestic science, asking local councils to appoint committees to communicate with her regarding domestic science in schools in their districts. Up to that time, only Ontario and Nova Scotia had done so, and, as convenor for the Standing Committee on Household Science, Adelaide felt it was vitally important to have information on a national scale. By the time the convention ended, Adelaid had also become provincial vice-president for Ontario.

Back home, she wrote to Harcourt expressing deep disatisfaction with Lilllian Massey Treble. Several months earlier, she had been impressed with Mrs. Treble's efforts in establishing domestic science classes in Toronto. Now Adelaide asked, "what has she or her school done for the cause?"[18] For the second time, Harcourt was asked to give preference to graduates of the Hamilton school when hiring domestic science teachers. Again, Adelaide's request was refused. Unlike the first instance, Harcourt did not even bother to reply personally; instead, Deputy-Minister John Millar wrote explaining it would be impossible to recognize Hamilton alone, since both Adelaide's and Mrs. Treble's schools were certified. One can only guess at Adelaide's fury on receiving that response.

Nevertheless, she made the best of it. On August 1st, she asked permission to attend a conference in Lake Placid. By the time she was back at home in September, Harcourt was writing to ask for help in planning Macdonald Institute:

What I would wish you decide would be the space required, dimensions of rooms, etc. You could say to me we want one room such a size, another room another size, etc.[19]

Adelaide, of course, was delighted to help out.

For some time, she had been thinking of resigning from the YWCA, largely because of her many domestic science duties. She tendered her resignation at the twelfth annual meeting on September 30th, and promised to remain deeply interested in the activities of the Association. She was immediately made honourary president, "in recognition of her untiring efforts and faithful services in connection with the work of the YWCA."[20]

The Niagara Escarpment which dominated Hamilton turned from green to scarlet and gold as the summer turned to fall. Adelaide had another reason to celebrate in early October, when Richard Harcourt announced the upgrading of domestic science qualifications for teachers. "The Normal school certificates will lapse after a certain time unless higher domestic science branches be mastered,"[21] a newspaper article reported. Adelaide was thrilled.

The above clipping was read with intense satisfaction and may I presumably thank you for such a wise move? The early teachers of D. S [sic] are not sufficiently equipped and to those following the growth of the question, such inefficiency means much injury to the cause as a factor in education. The MacDonald [sic] College will offer every facility in a post-graduate course— second to none in America.[22]

By requiring domestic teachers to upgrade their qualifications, the government had virtually guaranteed the success of Macdonald Institute.

For Adelaide, the government's action was the last major triumph of the year, a victory whose sweetness faded as she faced a series of difficult problems.

Chapter Fifteen

Trials and Tantrums

In late October, finances were again the topic of discussion in a letter
to Harcourt. In this instance, though, Adelaide seems to have been in excellent humour.

> As you were looking very tired yesterday, I thought it might relieve your
> mind somewhat to learn that at last I have mastered a typewriter sufficiently to remove the strain of deciphering my handwriting.[1]

She had just obtained the typewriter that morning and was thrilled with
it. In his reply, Harcourt congratulated her on her progressiveness: "You
are plucky indeed to learn typewriting. I am not surprised, since this one
of your many attributes has been appreciated by me for a long time."[2]

A certain daring and willingness to take advantage of new technology
was one of Adelaide's "good attributes." She learned typing as a means
of saving time, and, in the same spirit, she also learned to drive. And she
drove fast, according to a contemporary source. John, it seems, was more
cautious and never mastered the family automobile.

Unfortunately for the relationship between Harcourt and Adelaide the
novelty of the new typewriter soon wore off. In a letter dated November
19th she poured out her concerns. Although she conceded it was possible that illness might be magnifying the problem, she said she had been
horrified to receive a letter from a domestic science teacher inquiring
whether she was still involved in the organization and supervision of classes
in the subject. The question arose after Mr. Leake, the provincial inspector
of manual training, visited the teacher's class and told her he was the inspector for domestic science. Adelaide confessed to Harcourt that something similar had occurred in Ottawa, 'accompanied with such discourtesy
as to give the impression that I was interfering with what was not my business.'"[3] At the time, Harcourt had reassured her. "I have always been led
to think... the supervision of the work as my special duty."[4]

Adelaide was aghast at the thought of a male inspector of domestic
s c i e n c e .

> I am not speaking on personal grounds, I assure you, when I say that
> even such a possibility evokes the righteous indignation of domestic
> science workers. Such an unprecedented arrangement, as a man inspector of domestic science, borders on the ludicrous.... the only place
> in which a man tried to organize and supervise D, S, [sic] was in St.
> Louis, where he made a terrible muddle of the matter.[5]

She was hurt that, after so much "loyalty to the cause"[6] she had been placed in an "anomalous position."[7] She had no objection to Albert Leake visiting the classes, she said, and it would be useful to know how things were progressing between her own visits to the various schools. But she was concerned that her position be made clear, since she knew she had enemies. "No worker who puts the cause first can please every body."[8] She reassured Harcourt that she had no personal grudge against Leake. While it was commonly felt that women could not conduct professional relationships without allowing personal issues to intervene, Adelaide said, "I can not only work with, but admire people for whom I entertain the greatest personal indifference."[9]

Harcourt hastily replied to Adelaide's letter, advising her, "we must have no trouble over the inspection of classes in the different branches of Technical Education."[10] Consequently, Adelaide was apologetic in her next letter:

> Many thanks for your kind letter, which was doubly appreciated when you failed to give me the reproof which would have been justified by my "pettish" letter. But doubtless you recognized the evidence of a disturbed physical and mental condition. I have been quite ill, a sort of nervous breakdown — the first time I learned that I had nerves, with limitations — but am rapidly gaining lost ground. The last year has been unusually trying as you know, and I suppose it is a sort of reaction after the tension has been removed.[11]

Indeed, it has been a difficult year, and Adelaide's nervous energy had been strained to the limit before two sources of tension were removed. The Hamilton Board of Education established domestic science programmes, and John was about to launch a new business in his old premises, with Adelaide as a provisional director of the firm. While their financial situation was not quite what it once had been, there was great optimism that things would eventually straighten out.

By mid-December, however, Adelaide experienced another bitter disappointment. A cheque for $100 arrived from the Department of Education, bringing the total of Adelaide's yearly income to $600. She immediately wrote to Harcourt on the matter, and her letter reveals that her family finances were not the main consideration. Basically, Adelaide wanted more money as a token of official recognition for her contribution to domestic science education.

> Did I believe that you have not understood the situation, or the amount of work & responsibility entailed, I should not question the matter. Since last December I have given all my time — working time — to the cause of Domestic Science. The reorganization of the training school, and the worries & responsibilities attached, have been no light burden, you know the antagonistic element against which we have had to contend in Hamilton & which has been— I trust to overcome. The raising of money to make the school efficient, which I have had to do single-handed and for which, I venture to say, not a man in Canada would do gratuitously.

Muriel Hoodless and Adelaide Hoodless, ca. 1905.

The study and time given to working out the building & plan of work for the Guelph College. The very large correspondence which occupies a great deal of time & in order to make it satifactory, purchased a typewriter, although in the agreement made with Mr. Ross I was allowed to have clerical help when required, but which I have not taken advantage of [sic]. The inspection of classes, and making out of equipments, courses of study &c., has meant much time and thought, and surely it is not unreasonable to set a higher value on services, backed by ten years experience, — practically gratuitous to the Department until this year, when financially unable, I have spent more in investigating methods in other countries, and in getting the training school started, than I received in renumeration for services. It does not seem just, that the one who has had to stand the brunt of the battle, — as a pioneer has to do — met all sorts of opposition and in the face of ignorance of the question, succeeded in securing a recognized place for the new education in the minds of the public — should be placed in the same class— in value of services— as a graduate of the school over which she has presided & raised funds for the education of teachers. Our students are commanding good salaries, without any experience, and I do not feel that it is quite fair to be placed in the same list. This ability to present the subject to an audience, should surely stand for something over the ordinary teachers qualifications, and as yet I have not had one adverse press criticism but have carried my point to a standing vote on every occasion. I should certainly not have given the time to the matter, as I have in the last year, had I knot [sic] believed it was my duty, in the face of your assurance that I should be paid a good salary. I venture to say that there is not a man associated with the Department, with anything like the responsible duties I have to perform, who would be willing to be placed at such a low valuation. Therefore, as I have had very heavy obligations to meet this year, I feel sure you will forgive me for laying the matter before you from my point of view.[12]

Adelaide's disjointed train of thought and spelling and grammatical errors reflect the agitation she was feeling. She insisted it was not merely a question of money. She did not threaten to quit, for, as she explained, she felt it vital to continue her work.

Adelaide had obviously never accepted thr truism that there's no irreplaceable man— or woman, as she told Harcourt that if she stopped the work "all would be lost."[13] But she explained her reasoning in detail.

I know the Canadians in the field & there is not one to whom I should like to trust — what seems almost myself — the organization of this work just now. This may seem egotistical, but I assure you, it is not self or self-appreciation but an honest interest in the cause, and knowing its needs after years of experience.[14]

She repeated her dissatisfaction with the payment of a $600 fee, which was approximately the same salary as a public school domestic science teacher received. "It is almost 'infra dig' to accept a recognition equal only to our graduates in the public school work, & much below any in the more responsible positions.''[15]

As always, Adelaide expressed her misgivings at having to discuss money at all, and the hope that soon such discussions would not be necessary, an allusion, perhaps, to her desire for a permanent position with the Department. Nevertheless, necessity overcame her misgivings. As the person responsible for a training school

> ...which has so far provided all teachers in charge of public schools, Farmers' Institutes, etc., in the Province, apart from other duties, and the fact that it has been a year of planning for future results.... I do not think one thousand ($1000) dollars is too much for services requiring such a variety of qualifications. And in Domestic Science I feel equally at home in teaching a class — which you may not know I can do.... In the United States the organizers of D. S, [sic] get anywhere from $1500 to $3000 a year. I give you these facts to show that I have not asked the maximum by any means. I have depended on receiving at least the amount mentioned and that I was disappointed, just at this time, is putting it mildly.[16]

Despite the complaints, Adelaide's financial situation was not severe enough to give up holiday social activities. That month she attended a "golf ball club" held at the Royal Hotel, to which she wore a grey silk dress trimmed with pink. Other festivities were on her schedule as well, including, in all likelihood, a YWCA reception on December 30th.

If she did attend the reception, it was her last pleasant encounter with the YWCA. On January 13th, the Association held its annual meeting. What happened at this gathering of Christian women made headlines in the city newspapers. *The Hamilton Evening Times* reported "A Warm Time Among the Ladies At the Annual Meeting Yesterday— Mrs. Hoodless Left Out.''[17]

Organizational changes had taken place in the YWCA the previous September . Among those changes was a rule requiring the annual meeting be held in January, and that, rather than electing executives, a Board of Directors be elected. The main business of the January meeting, therefore, was to elect the Board of Directors, and it was decided that thirty positions would be available.

The meeting began at three o'clock, with the biggest attendance the Hamilton Association had ever witnessed. Fifty women were nominated for the Board of Directors, including Adelaide. The process of voting and counting ballots took so long that, by seven o'clock when the results were about to be announced, most of the women had left. Rev. F. E. Howitt and Mr. A.I. Mackenzie had been appointed scrutineers, and now read the results. Almost before the last name was announced all hell broke loose

> Mr. Mackenzie had barely finished reading the last name when Mrs. Hoodless broke out with considerable warmth. She said the result of the

vote was "a disgrace to a Christian association.... If the women who have never contributed more than a dollar to the institution should be put at the head of it, and those who have spent years of their lives are turned out, I say it is a disgrace, and I am ashamed of this institution."[18]

The *Spectator* gave a slightly different version of Adelaide's comments, but retained the emotional tone:

...'If women who have never given $1 or one hour's work to the association, are to receive the high vote indicated, while those who have spent years of hard work, to say nothing of the money they have also spent in the interest of the institution, are to be ignored, I'm ashamed of you."[19]

Enraged, she turned on the former president, who was now on the Board. "Miss Smith, remember when you go to take charge of this building that I will see that you refund the money that I have put into it."[20] It seemed nothing could stop Adelaide, who said she did not intend "to stand idly by and see the opposing faction carry out their cowardly mischief making.... People who would do a thing like this are beneath contempt."[21]

Several of Adelaide's supporters protested that they had voted for her. "But that lady was not appeased and bounced out of the building bristling with indignation."[22]

There was some suggestion that the meeting had been "packed" — that the anti-Hoodless faction had made sure relative newcomers to the YWCA would attend the meeting, and, by voting, ensure that she did not get a seat on the Board of Directors. Despite Adelaide's widely publicized temper tantrum, there was some demonstration of sympathy for her position. The day after the fracas was reported, one newspaper carried a letter suggesting the women who were not voted onto the Board should consider themselves lucky to have escaped "such a den of sedition."[23] After deploring the fact that members of the Association had not been more alert to approaching troubles, "Reader" stated

That the friends of the genial secretary [Jessie Campbell] have had it in for Mrs. Hoodless is quite evident, and few will say she did not deserve better treatment; and I venture to assert that the majority of our citizens — even those who in the past have indulged in a little criticism of the talented promoter of domestic science — will join in the conclusion that she deserved more consideration at the hands of some of her old colleagues.[24]

While she was still smarting from the rejection by the YWCA, Adelaide wrote to Harcourt asking for a meeting. She wanted to discuss the details of Macdonald Institute's organization. Harcourt's reply was cool. "I do not intend to interfere with the arrangements at Guelph."[25]

It would seem, given Harcourt's coolness and Adelaide's warmth, that the Minister had reluctantly met her demands for additional payment for her 1902 duties, but Harcourt seems to have become rather exasperated with Adelaide at this point. After she sent him her expense account on February 16th, he was required to write back to her asking that, in future, she make sure that items pertaining to Guelph be removed. The school was under the jurisdiction of the Department of Agriculture, an arrangement which would inevitably cause Adelaide some anxiety.

There was continuing friction between Adelaide and Harcourt because of her requests for a permanent position. She admitted her physical condition had something to do with her insistence. "'in justice to my self respect & nerves I cannot stand it any longer.''[26] She confessed that she had tried hard to see Harcourt's point of view:

> In doing so I have reasoned in this way, — that there were not enough centres of Domestic Science established to warrant the appointment of an official for that special work, and that it might be a political error to create an office without sufficient reason, and altogether the way does not seem very clear, so better postpone the matter as long as possible.[27]

While she could sympathize with his concerns, she could not easily accept his position. And she was worried, she said, at the fact that Macdonald Institute would not be connected with the Department of Education. So she suggested that she might act as a link between the Department of Education and Agriculture if she were appointed Director of Domestic Science.

> As I have no authority to do anything, and do not like to be continually "nagging" it seems to me that you would be relieved of much of the responsibility, & better work could be done if some one were made responsible.... If you will only have a little more confidence in me & give me a fair trial, I am sure it will be more satisfactory for all concerned. I have been in the work for ten years, and not once, in that time, have I had any difficulty with capable workers. The incapables do not like me, because I put the cause before personal considerations.[28]

Adelaide told Harcourt she had discussed the matter with George Ross, who seemed in favour of such an appointment and she was convinced that the Minister of Agriculture would also agree. But Harcourt's approval was essential, and this is what she now required.

Harcourt was adamant in his refusal. "You have forgotten that you assured me on more than one occasion that you were not looking for a permanent appointment, but that for special financial reasons you wished for a temporary appointment,''[29] he reminded her. Once more he offered to pay for inspection tours and speaking engagements, ''On the understanding that your appointment in such a capacity is to be considered merely temporary. I am not prepared at present to recommend your appointment, or the appointment in such a capacity of anyone indeed as Director of Domestic Science.''[30] Still, regardless of these limitations, he expressed appreciation of her work.

Although Adelaide tended to have an inflated opinion of her own worth in respect to domestic science, Harcourt could not very well sever his relationship with her, since much of the advice she gave him was sound. Often she reached conclusions based on intuition rather than careful analysis, and so her observations were sometimes flawed, but she probably had the best grasp of the overall condition of domestic science education in Canada at the time. For instance, she informed Harcourt that she often received letters from domestic science teachers who felt isolated because of lack of local advisors. Additionally, she cautioned him at least three times that it would not be advisable to form a committee to establish a curriculum for domestic science, even if the committee were made up of qualified teachers, since "each have received their training in different institutions and each claim superiority for that particular method."[31] It would be far better, she felt, to modify one of the curricula used in Britain or the US for Canadian use. If he chose to follow this route, Adelaide had three "approved by the best authorities"[32] which she could recommend.

Although Harcourt could not meet all of Adelaide's demands— and likely did not wish to — he did continue to use her to promote domestic science. By this time, however, more and more people were jumping on the bandwagon, which may explain an incident which occurred after Adelaide made an appearance in Ingersoll. Domestic science was an idea whose time had come, and the Ingersoll Board of Education soon established it in its public schools. Adelaide, quite naturally, claimed credit for this success, something which infuriated Albert Leake. The technical education inspector claimed that the success was the result of two speeches he had given in the town, and if anyone was going to claim the victory, he should.

Leake's antagonism may have been justified, since Adelaide was not above rearranging the facts to make herself appear in the best light. (This may also explain why critical newspaper reports and editorials are a rarity among the Hoodless family papers, although Adelaide seems to have saved every laudatory comment which appeared in print. While it is possible that the negative material was removed by her daughter or granddaughter, it is just as likely that Adelaide simply did not bother to save any report which emphasized her flaws.)

Ignoring this tendency for a moment, it is important to realize that Adelaide had been a major force in popularizing domestic science education. Certainly she was not the only person interested in technical education for boys and girls, and not the only one working to establish domestic science education in schools. But she was the most outspoken, and one of the most adept at drawing attention to the cause, and probably more closely connected with government than anyone outside bureaucrats and politicians. Her contribution cannot be minimized, regardless of her personal shortcomings. And, because she was certainly aware of the magnitude of her contribution, she must have had very mixed feelings as her years of work paid off while others demanded their share of the glory. Particularly galling to her was the increasing involvement of men in the cause, for it had been male officialdom which had held back the progress of domestic science for so long. Now that the subject was recognized as an important component of education, many of these same men were not only becoming known as advocates of the subject — they were being well paid for it!

Adelaide did not allow any bitterness she may have felt to stop her involvement in her favourite cause. And certainly the outward composure that years of speechmaking had given her served well. For example, when Governor and Lady Minto visted Hamilton that spring, a public reception was given. John and Adelaide were among the hundreds of guests in attendance, most of whom were awed by the vice-regal couple. ''When it came to the crucial moment some of the people seemed to be stricken with stage fright.''[33] Adelaide had no such qualms during her own presentation.

During this visit, Lady Minto and the Governor-General took in various points of interest in Hamilton, including the Ontario Normal School of Domestic Science and Art. Outside the building they were greeted by John Hoodless and Adam Brown, a prominent Hamilton business man. Inside, Adelaide conducted a tour of the premises after reading a welcoming speech.[34]

Buoyed by the approval of the representative of the crown, Adelaide decided to approach Harcourt again regarding her appointment as Director of Domestic Science.

> .... It does not seem wise to have Household Science organized from the teachers' point of view alone, and for this reason, if for no other, I should like to have some control of the work for a time.
> .... The matter of salary I shall leave to those with whom I have to deal. As I should like to give more time to the work, and as I owe my family some compensation for duties which are strictly mine, I trust that a sufficient salary will be allowed to dignify the position and make it worth working for in the future.[35]

Unfortunately for Adelaide, Richard Harcourt could be as persistent as she. Despite her pleading, he again refused to consider the appointment.

Chapter Sixteen

Macdonald Institute

The removal of the teacher's college to Guelph in 1903 meant the building at 17 Main Street was now available for other purposes. The use of the school was offered to the Board of Education, along with all the equipment. It is important to note here that, although the Board of Education referred to the offer as coming from the "management" of the School of Domestic Science and Arts, it was referring to the YWCA, which owned the school building, and not to the school itself, of which Adelaide was president. It seems Adelaide had severed her connection with the YWCA completely, and was now concentrating on making Macdonald Institute a success.

The building was far from complete, due, in part, to labour strikes, but classes were scheduled to begin that fall. Meanwhile, Adelaide, James Mills, and others were doing what they could to assure the success of the school. Sir William had already added $50,000 to this original donation, but the school would need as much money as could possibly be raised. Thus, on 5 October, James Mills wrote to Adelaide asking her to take along "a statement of things I think we should aim at"[1] on her forthcoming trip to Montreal.

> I think it is well to aim high, even if we accomplish nothing. There is no doubt that the Institute would be much more efficient and successful if it could be managed so as to have it largely independent of annual votes by the legislature.[2]

Among the things Mills was aiming at was an endowment for scholarships and the erection of a small hospital. The latter was needed, he said, "both to take charge of those who may be sick and also to furnish the necessary instruction in home nursing and emergencies."[3]

Adelaide, of course, did what she could to persuade Sir William that the plan was a good one, and, slowly, the new school took shape.

Macdonald Institute, as it was called, was located on twelve acres north of the college campus. Although the Guelph Street railway ran nearby, the site offered a pleasant view of trees and countryside.

The Institute itself was a three-storey brick and terra cotta structure containing classrooms "for the practical training in Nature Study, Manual Training and Household Sciences."[4] A second building, Macdonald Hall, contained kitchens, a dining room, as well as a gymnasium and other facilities for recreation, and would serve as residence for up to one hundred women.

Macdonald Institute, Guelph, Ontario.

By August 1903, a provincial announcement had been published outlining the courses of study at the Institute. There was a three-month course for qualified teachers who wished to augment their knowledge of domestic science. A one year homemaker's course covered the usual domestic science topics, along with physics, chemistry, and biology. This was called the "diamond ring" course, possibly because so many of its graduates quickly became engaged or married.

A two-year course was also offered to women who intended to teach domestic science. In addition to the curriculum covered in the one year course, it included Math, History, and two electives from Home Dairying, Poultry, Horticulture, Seeds and Plant Improvement or Woodcarving. Tuition was set at $45 per year for all the courses, or $15 per three-month term, but the prospective students were advised that board and laundry costs would raise their expenses to around $60 per term.

The ability to pay the tuition was not the only requirement for entrance to domestic science courses. Graduates were expected to be ambassadors for the Institute, especially if they went to work as teachers or professional housekeepers. Consequently, applicants were carefully screened. Students had to be at least 17 and were required to pass four entrance exams: Reading, Writing and Dictation, English Grammar; Elements of Arithmetic; Outline of General Geography, and Geography of Canada. Moreover, they were also required to produce satisfactory evidence as to moral character and physical health."[5] An entry in the Institute calendar for the year 1904-05 stated,

> Applicants for this course must be mature women in sound health with executive ability and with sufficient education to do readily the necessary marketing and office work, and with considerable experience in practical housework.[6]

To allay any parental fears, the girls who lived at Macdonald Hall were carefully supervised by a housemother. Discipline was of paramount importance, although at a minimum age of 17 most of the students could be considered adults, and several of them were already supporting themselves. Nevertheless

> Students are required to render cheerful and willing obedience to orders, to conduct themselves in an orderly manner at all times, to avoid noisy or boisterous conduct, to observe neatness of dress on the street and at prayers, meals and lectures, and to keep their rooms neat and tidy.[7]

In spite of the emphasis on discipline, students developed a strong sense of camaraderie, and school regulations would not dampen their spirits. A writer who visited the Institute recounted how the girls gleefully chanted:

> Make 'em, Bake 'em! Make 'em—Bake 'em! Boil 'em,-Broil 'em-Sew, Not a soul who ever comes here Ever wants to go. Here we learn to run

our houses, Here we learn to say,— "Three times three for old Macdonald, Tiger now, Hurray!"[8]

Even before the school's formal opening, classes were held in any available space. One report described how sewing classes were held in the library under the direction of the school's principal, Mary Urie Watson.

Adelaide lectured on "Ethics and the Home," a required part of the course of studies at the Institute. To a great extent, her course comprised her own beliefs on the sanctity of the home and woman's proper sphere. These were topics she had frequently discussed as part of her missionary work, and in many instances she simply recycled reports and speeches for classroom use.

Her introductory lecture discussed the definition of ethics, the fact that it had been traditionally approached from a male viewpoint, and the necessity of incorporating ethics— which Adelaide viewed as a compound of religious conviction and character building— into the management of Canadian homes.

> In "Education and the Higher Life" Prof. Henderson tells us that "the only sane purpose in life, is the quest of perfection." As we want Macdonald Institute to represent not only sanity of purpose, but an avenue by which at least a degree of perfection may be reached, we must have it in those elements which make for the unfolding and perfecting of the human spirit. We have been told that "it is better to idealize the real than to realize the ideal." And as this school stands for an ideal home — which represents the things already in existence — and for the education of the home-maker, it is essential that this ideal should be based on sound principles.... We want this school to stand for the highest type of womanhood. I have tried in this introductory talk, to make clear to you, the aim of the school, and we ask your cooperation in the fulfilment of that purpose. As you represent the school in your daily lives, will its influence extend or diminish. As pioneers of the new education for women, you will be closely watched. To those who are going out as teachers I would especially emphasize the importance of directing your pupils towards the higher aims of life, as well as to the performance of the more practical duties. The great need in our schools today is character building. Honor and courtesy, are sadly lacking in the average Canadian youth, and until the same standard of manners and morals is established for the home and the school, and parents and coworkers with the teachers, it will be impossible to harmonize social influence for the ultimate goal of humanity.[9]

If her listeners managed to stay awake during what was a rather long and tedious speech, one wonders if they agreed with Adelaide's statement that they would be closely watched. Did the burden of responsibility for the future of Canadian homes weigh heavily on them? It seems more likely that the students, like many young people, may have made fun of Adelaide behind her back, even if they appreciated her concerns.

Adelaide's position at the Institute, along with the continued association with the provincial government, necessitated some unusual tasks from time to time. In early 1904, she carried on some correspondence with Richard Harcourt regarding a Mrs. MacDonald at Lambton Mills, Ontario. Apparently the lady in question "nearly drove us out of our senses at the Home Science Section of the O.E.A."[10] Mrs. MacDonald was a cooking teacher who wanted a position as a teacher of domestic science, and had written to Harcourt to discover why her name was not on a list of candidates. Harcourt asked Adelaide to clear up the matter. While remarking to the Minister of Education that "there is every reason to be thankful that her name was not put on the list of teachers,"[11] Adelaide was slightly more courteous in her letter to the lady in question.

> There are many positions open in private schools and other institutions where the work is of a more utilitarian character, and cookery is the chief object, but a pedagogical training is absolutely necessary now for the public and high school work. Trusting that I have made the matter clear to you and regretting that you should feel ill used in regard to your former communication, of which no record can be found, and which I assure you, could not be intentional, I remain, very truly yours.... [12]

Once more, Adelaide had managed to stress the importance of extensive training in domestic science without recognizing her own paradoxical situation. And, by this time, she had many critics who were more than willing to point out her lack of training. "It is not only her lack of science but her lack of mental training that makes Mrs. Hoodless incapable of real first class academic work,"[13] Alice Chown, Secretary of the Canadian Household Economics Association complained to Richard Harcourt. There were rumblings that Adelaide was doing the cause of domestic science education in Canada more harm than good. Now that qualified North American teachers of the subject were on the increase, Adelaide's obvious lack of education was an embarrassment, especially when coupled with her unflagging belief in her own expertise. She had, in the words of one observer, "zeal without discretion."[14]

Nevertheless, her assistance was still welcomed by the government and directors of the Macdonald Institute. When George Creelman succeeded James Mills as president of the Ontario Agricultural College, he continued to rely on Adelaide's input.

> I wish to thank you for the continued interest you are taking in the work of the Macdonald Institute. Dr. Mills informs me that you have been most helpful to him, and I am in hopes that you will favor me to the same extent. As regards the china, linen, and so forth for the Residence, I would be very glad if at this time you would give me, with as much detail as possible, a statement of what will be required. We will then be in a position to go fully into the matter, with a view to take definite action at an early date.... [15]

That was in May. By August, another crisis had developed: her course had been removed from the curriculum of Macdonald Institute.

W.H. Muldrew, the first dean of the Institute, was responsible for the cancellation. Possibly he had been in contact with trained domestic science teachers who had pointed out Adelaide's shortcomings; possibly, the former high school teacher observed them for himself. Whatever the case, Adelaide was crushed. She apparently wrote to OAC president George Creelman and Macdonald Institute principal Mary Watson to find out whether they were involved in the action. Both assured her they were not, for, on 18 August, Adelaide wrote to Creelman:

> Many thanks for your kind letter, which I felt would come when you understood matters. I could not associate you, or what I thought of you, with such injustice, and I am glad (more than I can express) that my confidence was not misplaced. I do not know which hurt the most, the fear that you and Miss Watson were capable of treating me so, or the deprivation of any further part in the future of Macdonald.[16]

She complained at feeling left out because she had not been consulted regarding announcements of Macdonald Institute's plans for the immediate future. "No one likes to have the work of years simply ignored, especially when so many are looking forward to me for the recognition of their training and position in the field."[17] Apparently the arrangement had been made for graduates of the Ontario Normal School of Domestic Science and Art to be considered as alumnae of the Institute, since the latter had effectively incorporated the Normal school. This was important, Adelaide felt, since it prevented the Normal school graduates from losing prestige.

But what really rankled was the cancellation of her course. She reiterated her strong feelings on the subject of ethics before bringing religion into the matter for extra leverage:

> One student said to me, "it was the only subject which brought us into touch with Divine dealings, as we do not even have an opening prayer in the school." Now my dear Mr. Creelman I am too firm a believer in the power of divine guidance to believe that the highest blessing will come where such matters are ignored. That is why I should like to continue my studies with the students....[18]

Only Adelaide would threaten divine retribution as a penalty for the cancellation of her course!

As Adelaide herself suggested, the cancellation was probably not as upsetting as the suspicion that she would be cut off from contact with Macdonald Institute. To prevent this, she pointed out how useful she could be to the staff:

> I am in the outside world more than any of the lady members of the staff, and can keep them in touch with what is going on in other fields.... whatever I learn from other schools from my wanderings, I give her

[Mary Watson] the benefit of.... I always felt that it would be a mistake to let the school fall into the hands of teachers, without someone to look after the home point of view.... I feel that Dr. Muldrew has no right to drive me from doing what has been pronounced by much better authorities than he, a move in the right direction and in which I feel I can be of use to the cause. It means hard work for me but after fifteen years of work it would kill me to give up entirely. Honestly I never had anything upset my nerves and health so much as the recent shock, and its possible consequences.[19]

Adelaide asked Creelman for constructive criticism and pleaded that he not involve Richard Harcourt in the matter. Perhaps she suspected Harcourt would be willing to let the matter rest, rather than supporting her bid for reinstatement. She also urged Creelman to allow her to continue her work with the Institute, which, she hoped, would prevent it from becoming a "teacher factory."[20]

Was Adelaide beginning to feel she had created a monster? She does not seem to have appreciated the scope of Macdonald Institute, which, in addition to teaching domestic science, would provide nature study courses and other training for teachers of rural schools. She was disappointed that the University of Toronto, as well as Macdonald Institute, was empowered to grant certificates to teachers of domestic science. Most importantly, she seems to have felt her homely idea had got completely out of hand. She had envisioned a system by which girls could be taught the skills needed to run a home, care for a family, and contribute to society by setting an example of unselfish devotion. Teachers, ideally, would combine formal training in the latest methods of domestic science and art with the womanly attributes Adelaide held dearest: a sense of duty, a loving maternalism, a refined morality, and a conviction that the home was the foundation of society. Except for the fact that she lacked a diploma from a recognized educational institution, Adelaide seems to have been convinced that she was the ideal teacher for such courses. Lacking the same grounding in ethics which she herself possessed, and which she attempted to transmit to students at Macdonald, new graduates of domestic science "became too materialistic, and instead of developing the more distinct feminine characteristics, it tends to make them mechanical."[21] She became increasingly bitter, and extremely sensitive to criticism, real or imagined. However, she had one source of satisfaction regarding her lectures in Guelph, albeit a morbid one. Muldrew died of diptheria, and Adelaide resumed her lectures. In view of her comments to Creelman, one wonders if she looked on Muldrew's demise as an example of heavenly justice.

The formal opening of Macdonald Institute took place in early December. George Creelman officiated at the ceremony, which was attended by Dr. Mills, Professor Robertson, and Agricultural Minister John Dryden. Adelaide was also present, and made a short speech. In essence the speech echoed the convictions she expressed in her course on ethics:

It was to build up character as well as develop the mentality that the Macdonald Institute was founded. This was a school for the making of home makers and no nobler work could be allotted to any institution.[22]

It's easy to imagine the looks of dismay being exchanged by some members of the staff on hearing comments like this. The persistence, singlemindedness, and refusal to give up which had been assets in Adelaide's fight for domestic science had now become liabilities, at least in the minds of many of her associates. She continued to work in the field, and her reputation as an educational pioneer seems to have been undiminished among the general public. But Adelaide's career had peaked with the founding of the Ontario Normal School for Domestic Science and Art. The establishment of the Macdonald Institute was a triumph, certainly, but it was not hers alone. After the official opening, her career seems to have taken a slow but definite downward trend.

Chapter Seventeen

Trade School Advisor

Early in 1905, Adelaide fell ill once again. Although this seems to have been a second nervous breakdown, there is some evidence that physical ailments were also threatening her health. She had grown increasingly stout over the years, and it is possible that she suffered from high blood pressure or heart problems. Whatever her physical condition, however, Adelaide's mental attitude seems to have had a much greater influence over her life.

The bittersweet nature of her victories in domestic science education were a continuing source of irritation, and she was particularly annoyed at the fact that it seemed easier for men to achieve goals that had eluded her. "It seems hard that women have to fight for every inch of justice for their work, and when men ask for a thing it is granted without our side being so much as consulted." [1]

Whether it was her disappointment at what she perceived as a betrayal by those she had helped, or her uncertain health, over the next five years Adelaide was rather less active in public life. Certainly she continued to inspect schools and speak before interested groups on the merits of domestic science, and, increasingly, on technical education. But the spotlight was less frequently directed at her. Possibly this was because domestic science had become an accepted part of Canadian education. More likely it was due to the increased number of workers in the field, many of whom held opinions which conflicted with Adelaide's.

It might have been better for Adelaide to retire from public life altogether at this point, to rest on her laurels. Despite criticism, she was still highly regarded in many circles and could easily have basked in the glow of her achievements while leaving the work to younger, better educated successors. As Adelaide herself suggested, domestic science education was now so much a part of her that she could not contemplate life without it. Furthermore, at this point, she needed domestic science more than it needed her, for her family was grown and it would not be long before they all left home.

In 1905, Bernard graduated from the Ontario Agricultual College at the age of 20. He went to work exhibiting cattle and managing farms in southern Ontario and New York State. Edna, like her mother, was an enthusiastic golfer. At 23 she was well known as a gifted amateur player, and had won several tournaments. Muriel, the youngest of the three, was 19, and strongly resembled her mother. Like Edna and many young women of the day, Muriel probably spent a good deal of time attending social functions in hopes of finding a husband.

But it was Edna who married first. Her marriage to Henry Montgomery Bostwick, a young executive with Westinghouse, was one of the social events of the autumn of 1907. The Hamilton newspapers ran lengthy articles on the wedding, which took place at 3 p.m. on the afternoon of 9 October at the Church of the Ascension. Canon Wade, a long time family friend, officiated.

The guests came from near and far, supporting the *Evening Times* statement that Edna was "one of Hamilton's most charming and popular daughters."[2] Dressed in "a lovely gown of white liberty satin with trimmings of Brussels point-de-rose and chiffon, the tulle veil being worn over a coronal of orange blossoms,"[3] Edna carried a cascade of roses, and was given away by her father.

Muriel was among the maids of honour, wearing "shell pink chiffon voile"[4] and a hat trimmed with pink ostrich feathers. Bernard was present, too, as an usher.

For the first of her children's weddings, Adelaide had dressed with special care. "Mrs. Hoodless, mother of the bride, wore a chic gown of pale mauve embroidered marquisette, with Brussels point-de-rose lace, mauve satin and applique, mauve hat with orchids and shaded ostrich feathers, bouquet of orchids."[4] Following the ceremony, Adelaide and John hosted a reception at Eastcourt, which had been lavishly decorated with flowers for the occasion. Afterwards, the newlyweds left for a honeymoon in the east, but Adelaide had the consolation of knowing Edna would be setting up her home in Hamilton.

With two of her adult chidren leading lives of her own, and the knowledge that her missionary work was all but done, Adelaide must have felt terribly bereft. She presented a brave front to the world: the competent Mrs. Hoodless, a devoted volunteer, an acknowledged expert in domestic science education, a woman with an enviable string of accomplishments to her credit. Privately, she agonized over the direction domestic science was taking and over her own diminishing influence. She was a stubborn woman, who gave the impression of unwavering confidence in her own theories. But she was neither stupid nor insensitive, and the awareness that there were many who thought her inept, ignorant, or inconsistent must have pained her far more than any previous opposition to domestic science.

Adelaide was no quitter, however. To sit on the sidelines without making any attempt to correct wrongs she perceived would have been anathema. She had to keep fighting, to draw what satisfaction she could from progress in domestic science education. One thing which must have pleased her greatly was the expansion of the domestic science programme in Hamilton schools. By November 1906, the Board of Education's Internal Management Commitee recommended the introduction of domestic science in two new schools. Three years later, there would be a total of

Wedding of Edna Hoodless and Henry Bostwick, 1907. Left to right: Muriel Hoodless, John Hoodless, Edna Hoodless Bostwick, Henry M. Bostwick, Adelaide Hoodless.

six domestic science teachers on the Board's payroll.

Adelaide's ideas about domestic science had changed very little since the beginning of her career. As late as 1907, in a report to the Dominion Educational Association, she listed the reasons why domestic science should be taught in the schools:

1. To give children an intelligent interest in and a wholesome regard for the occupations in the home.

2. To bring school and home into closer co-operation towards social ends.

3. To give the young pupils a knowledge of and a regard for elementary science by the scientific study of those common concerns of home life which may mean so little but should mean so much.

4. To make young persons more keenly conscious of the great importance of physical health and vigor and consequently mental health by due regard for diet, sanitation and right living.

5. To make pupils more intelligent regarding the procuring, transporting and preparation of food, clothing and shelter.

6. To impress patrons and children of the school with the usefulness and the worth, even in a physical sense, of education.

7. To afford relaxation from mental tasks by engaging the hands as well as the brains in the work of education, thus attending to the motor as well as the mental interests of the child.

8. Enabling children to be real social factors in the home by comparing quality, cost, and ways of preparing things in the home with similar facts learned at school thereby influencing parents to modify customary procedure towards something better and more economical.

9. To give the pupils a deeper personal regard for community interests and occupations in general, and the persons whose lives are identified with these.[5]

She ended her remarks by arguing that domestic science was the foundation on which a better society rested.

Does society as a whole show any need that such a study would meet and answer? Surely the most casual student of present social conditions must see that a large proportion of our population, both rich and poor, is in poor physical condition, and that there is in consequence great economic waste; for lack of vigor means lack of effective accomplishment, and also makes necessary large expenditure for remedial measures. With better shelter, food, water, ventilation, cleanliness and proper clothing, a check would be placed on this enormous waste, and more real work would be done, and there would be fewer patent medicines, patent foods, and hospitals. Another common waste is through poor buying and extravagant use of materials. To what are these things due? (1) ignorance of women on these points in the management of a household; (2) ignorance of men and women together in the management of that larger household, the city (or state)....   If all our citizens, both men and women. were alive to the physical and economic evils consequent on bad building, imperfect water supply, defective disposal of waste, and dirty streets, these things would not exist. The teaching of home economics should go far to correct these errors, for it emphasises health as a normal condition, and gives knowledge of the physical conditions which will maintain this; emphasises the home as the unit of society, and the management of the home as a business needing brains and special training; shows how, on the economic side of marriage the wife is the business partner, that her part as a spender and manager is no less important than the husband's as earner, and that he cannot succeed if she fails to meet her obligations.[6]

Adelaide continued to view domestic science education as the solution to most social ills. She was also convinced that women had no business in politics until they could manage their homes efficiently and well. It was not a belief which would win her many supporters among the most progressive women of the day, and, indeed, Adelaide's dogmatic approach to domestic science makes it seem almost miraculous that people listened to her at all. The reason for her success, of course, was her charm and her sense of humour, both of which rarely shone through in contemporary newspaper reports. For instance, on one occasion she was addressing an audience when someone asked about the expense of teaching domestic science. Adelaide replied, ''A great many people have asked, what do you do with all the things you make? Why, I said, we make very little in the first place, and, in the next place, we eat it.''[7] Any tension created up to that point disappeared in the audience's laughter.

Adelaide's humour may have helped ensure the loyalty of many of her supporters. In 1908, during an election campaign, an editorial appeared which told how Tory supporters had tried to get domestic science withdrawn from Hamilton schools. 'That they did not carry out their threat was only because such a strong expression of parental opinion was furnished them that they were obliged to desist.'[8]

In view of this public support, according to the editorial, it seemed wise for the Conservative candidate, J. J. Scott, to appear to be a strong advocate of technical education, including domestic science. ''To the people of Hamilton, who have never heard before anything of Mr. Scott's great interest in, and sacrifices for, technical education for girls, or boys either, this will be news indeed.''[9]

John Hoodless, a Tory himself, apparently challenged Scott's statement. He spoke briefly and politely on Adelaide's work, the editorial reported, and rightly so.

> In such circumstances it seems less than chivalrous for the speakers at the Tory convention to seek to steal from Mrs. Hoodless the laurels which she so well earned by her services to Hon. George Ross' Education Department to bedeck the brow of J. J. Scott.... And if Mr. John Hoodless had risen in righteous wrath to protest against this effort to glorify Scott by wronging Mrs. Hoodless in the matter, he would have

Later that year, Adelaide resigned from her National Council position as provincial vice-president and convenor of the Domestic Science Committee. The announcement was received with regret in many quarters, including London, Ontario, where a note was forwarded to the local newspaper.

> Having heard that Mrs Hoodless is about to resign office, the London Local Council takes this opportunity of expressing its regret. It also desires to place on record its appreciation of the great work she has done in the interest of Domestic Science in Ontario and throughout the Dominion.
> Since it was through Mrs. Hoodless that Sir William Macdonald's interest was first aroused in the subject, we also desire to congratulate her upon what is indirectly the crowning achievement of her strenuous and enthusiastic efforts— the establishment of Macdonald Hall, at Guelph, where, by Sir William's splendid beneficence, our young women are enabled to learn the handicrafts belonging to homemaking and home-keeping under the happiest auspices.''[11]

The previous year, the Women's Institute had celebrated its tenth anniversary. Out of gratitude to its founder, the women decided to finance the painting of Adelaide's portrait. A Toronto artist, John Wycliffe Lowes Forster, was commissioned. Forster's other sitters had included Alexander Graham Bell, Bliss Carmen, Timothy Eaton, and Sir John A. Macdonald. Since Adelaide knew Forster, and likely was acquainted with the prestigious list of earlier sitters, having her portrait done must have been highly flattering.

The finished canvas became the best known likeness of Adelaide to survive. It shows a woman of great determination, handsome and well-dressed, not precisely bitter, but rather saddened by the experiences of life. In many ways, the oil portrait shows a woman of more character than the young matron who posed for a photograph taken in 1887.

What Adelaide's reaction to the portrait was is not recorded. Her daughter Edna apparently thought it was well done. The artist, she said, ''... was able to put some of her charm on canvas.''[12] The portrait, which does not seem to be an overly idealized likeness, emanates much more warmth than most photographs taken during the same period. In most of these, Adelaide looks stern and forbidding. She may have felt self-conscious posing, except when lulled into relaxation by an amiable and skilled artist. Candid photos of this era, probably taken by Edna, show another facet of Adelaide: the doting mother smiling as Muriel teases a dog in the garden, the devoted wife laughing, almost flirtatiously, at some remark John has just made. Regardless of her problems in public life, Adelaide seems always to have relished her relationship with her family.

But various duties took her away from home on many occasions. Throughout 1908, Adelaide made many trips to Ontario schools, as well as to schools in the United States.

The provincial government was now looking into the question of technical education for girls— education to prepare them for work in the industrial sector— and Adelaide had been asked to report on American progress in this area.

In the autumn of 1908, Adelaide went to the United States, where she visited several schools, including the Carnegie Technical Schools in Pittsburgh, the Manhattan Trade School for Girls, the Hebrew Technical School for Girls in New York City, and the Pratt Institute in Brooklyn. Adelaide was an unlikely candidate as an advocate of technical eduction. Certainly the field was related to domestic science, in that the methods of teaching were vaguely similar, and many American trade schools offered domestic science as part of the curriculum. But, for Adelaide, domestic science would always remain paramount. In Pittsburgh, she urged students of the Margaret Morrison Carnegie School to

> go out from their schools as missionaries to reclaim young women from the commercialism of the day they would find in the making of homes for themselves and others a greater opportunity for happiness than working in offices or factories.[13]

Given these convictions, it is difficult to accept Adelaide as qualified to report on trade schools to the new Minister of Education, Dr. R. A. Pyne. Indeed, her report shows an amazing lack of understanding of the different types of trade schools:

> Technical schools occupy a position in relation to trade similar to the High School in relation to the professions. The object of the technical school is to train experts, master mechanics, etc.[14]

That definition was adequate, as was Adelaide's detailed description of other aims of technical schools:

> ...not to take the place of an enlightened apprenticeship, but rather to help those who already know something of a certain class of work and wish more scientific or theoretic knowledge of it. Technical schools, therefore, prepare the overseer or the superintendent rather than to fit a student directly for the trade. Night technical schools... often partake of the nature of supplementary trade schools, which supplement the knowledge which the student is obtaining in some trade workroom during the day.[15]

So far, so good. But Adelaide's attempts to define the aims of industrial and manual trianing schools were far less detailed.

> Industrial schools... aim to teach one or more branches of industry with the idea that habits of order and work will be inculcated. This form of school is often used for reformatory purpose. Manual training Schools

give hand work with the sole idea of utilizing the power in developing or educating the individual, that hand and mind may be trained together and help each other.[16]

Adelaide claimed to have followed the trade school issue very closely, "... through the various discussions which have taken place among manufacturers, Boards of Trade, special committees, and other organizations concerning technical education, as reported from time to time in the daily papers."[17] Yet she failed to grasp the differences between technical education and domestic science. To some extent this may have been because many of the subjects taught in trade schools were branches of what Adelaide considered domestic science, including cooking, sewing, designing, embroidery, and millinery. But Adelaide was also handicapped by her lifelong emphasis on housekeeping— either for her own family, or in a professional capacity— as the only worthwhile occupation for women. Emotionally, she could never place technical training on the same level as domestic science.

Nevertheless, she had been given a job to do, and she did it to the best of her ability. What she lacked in knowledge she made up for with emotional appeals to reform-minded citizens who felt compelled to improve the lot of the less fortunate. After pointing out that what technical education existed in Ontario schools was almost exclusively for boys, she wrote:

> It is a well known fact that about half of the pupils attending the public and high schools are girls, and a large majority of these girls must eventually become wage-earners.... That the circumstances compelled women to follow the various industries into shop and factory, without either mental or technical training, accounts, in a large measure, for the lower standard of efficiency, lower wages and consequent social deterioration of women wage-earners. That this is a serious social and economic matter is beyond question.[18]

She compared the progress of technical education in Canada with that in the United States, and as usual, the American system was further advanced.

> The extremely limited provisions made in a few [Canadian] schools for instruction in domestic science and sewing is all the consideration allowed for the vast army of women workers.... In the large technical schools in the United States, courses are offered for the training of women as directors in workrooms, teachers of the various trades open to women, librarians, secretaries, physical culture instructors, costume designers, illustrators, instructors in decorative and applied design, teachers of domestic science and sewing, and various other occupations.[19]

Typically, Adelaide saw education as a means of implementing far-reaching social reform, and explained why trade schools could not only improve the earning power of young women, but also reduce crime.

> What becomes of all the girls released from school at fourteen or fifteen years of age? What has the school done to make them of value to employers of labour? The home industries are limited and the active, self-dependent girl must seek employment elsewhere. What is her position socially and morally, during the years in which she is trying to acquire sufficient proficiency to earn a decent living wage?
>
> Statisticians and social reformers tell us that the criminal and social outcasts are largely recruited from this class. It is reasonable that such consequences should follow where struggling incompetence causes discouragement before sufficient skill is developed to command living wages. This is where the trade school comes in as an organized apprenticeship, enabling the pupil to learn a trade under social and moral conditions which will carry her through the two or three years, which may be called the transition period between girlhood and womanhood, and sending her into the field of labour, a self-respecting, intelligent worker, conscious of her duty to her employer and herself.
>
> The Trade School is the outcome of the various experiments in technical education, and is the extension of elementary education on the lines over which the majority of pupils attending the public schools will travel. The following explanation of what a trade school should be is given by the principal of a large Normal School in the United States.
>
> 1st — It must be a part of the public school.
>
> 2nd — It must be an evolution out of present conditions.
>
> 3rd — It must attempt to meet particular needs of the local community.
>
> 4th — It must be recognized as practical and helpful on the material side by the common people. In the rural school it should lead to a knowledge of farming, gardening, poultry raising, and other agricultural pursuits. In the manufacturing centres with the industries established, the result of such schools should be towards higher standards of living (not more elaborate) and the development of a more intelligent, earnest, and capable worker. In the smaller places it has been suggested that high schools should adjust their courses so as to meet the needs of the majority.[20]

During her visit to the United States, Adelaide also spread the word about Macdonald Institute. Members of the Carnegie Schools' administration were sufficiently interested to make a trip to Guelph to inspect the facilities. Impressed with the school Adelaide helped to establish, they offered her a position as advisor to the Carnegie Schools.

It is safe to assume that much of Adelaide's work involved reporting what she saw in other schools, and making recommendations based on her observations. It is also quite likely, given her difficult financial circumstances of earlier years, that Adelaide received a small stipend or honorarium in exchange for her advice.

Adelaide's appointment to an organization bearing the name of the famous philanthropist provoked a good deal of favourable comment in

Canada. The *Hamilton Spectator* was lavish in its praise:

> The women of Canada will feel pleased at the signal honor that has been conferred upon Mrs. Hoodless of this city, in being selected by the directors of the Carnegie Technical schools as one to advise and inspect the work which is being carried forward in these great institutions at Pittsburgh.... Mrs. Hoodless has been untiring in her efforts to advance this work in both Canada and the United States, and too much praise cannot be bestowed upon her for what she has done to better the conditions of the young women and girls who are compelled to support themselves in both countries.[21]

The *Hamilton Herald* also carried an announcement of Adelaide's appointment:

> A high tribute has been paid to Mrs. John Hoodless, of this city, by the directors of the Carnegie Technical schools of Pittsburgh, in her appointment as one of the advisors and inspectors of the work that is being carried on in them, and it is one which her many friends in this city will appreciate as being worthily bestowed.[22]

Once again, Adelaide was put in the public eye. Faced with the possibility of a new career, a new crusade, and a resurgence of public interest in her accomplishments, Adelaide must have felt revitalized. At this point, she probably had every expectation that her fifties would be as productive as her late thirties and forties had been.

Chapter Eighteen

"The Gratitude of the Citizens"

In June, the International Council of Women held its fifth Congress in Toronto. Although the Congress was given extensive coverage, especially in the Toronto, newspapers, hardly any mention was made of Adelaide. This may be attributable to the fact that, since domestic science had become better known and more widespread, it was less newsworthy. While Adelaide was head of the National Council's Standing Committee on Domestic Science and Technical Education, and chaired two sessions at the convention, the topic was of less concern to the International Council as a whole than the issues of world peace and female suffrage.

Still, the congress provided Adelaide with an opportunity to propound her views on domestic science and technical education. She continued to take every opportunity to do this, especially when she encountered powerful individuals. That autumn, she was a guest at a society wedding where she spoke to Sir Wilfred Laurier about technical and industrial education. Apparently the prime minister asked, "If you were a despot, what would you do?"[1]

Adelaide answered the question, but on reflection, decided she had not done so adequately. Consequently, on 3 November she elaborated her views in a letter to Laurier:

> If I were a despot— or Premier of Canada— I should encourage industrial and technical education by giving each Province a grant, or bonus, in proportion to the special requirements of each Province for the purpose of *stimulating* more interest in this phase of education in keeping with the develpment of our natural resources....
>
> Secondly, I would establish in Ottawa a Government School of Technology for research and experimental work. A school in which Canadian genius could be developed, at government expense if necessary, as in the National Laboratories of Germany. A school in which the brilliant students discovered and developed up to a certain point in the Provinces could be utilized for the national benefit and become a national asset. At the present time we are dependent upon other countries, where conditions are different, for leaders in any department of industrial development requiring a high degree of technical and scientific knowledge. That we have the human as well as the material resources has been demonstrated too often to require emphasis, but alas! Other countries notably our Southern neighbors too often reap the benefit....
>
> Believe me I am not presenting this matter from a sentimental or visionary point of view, but in consequence of many years of study and investigation of social and industrial conditions in Canada and other

countries. One point has been clearly brought out, that in every case where rapid advancement has been made, it has been due to the *stimulus* given by financial aid either from individuals or corporations. Indiviudal aid frequently follows national interest and vice versa. This was proved in our own special work. So long as the interest remained local little progress was made, but as soon as it became clear a legislative matter through the kind co-operation of the Hon. G. W. Ross, then Minister of Education, it assumed much larger and more vital proportions.[2]

Laurier replied promptly with a brief letter. "I am sorry to say that though Premier of Canada, I have no despotic power, which I sometimes regret, but which is far better for the people."[3] He explained that the federal government had recently granted additional funds to the province to aid in improving school systems. Regarding Adelaide's idea of a technical school in Ottawa, Laurier said,

> ...it would be opening a very large door and I think, on the whole, we had better leave education where the constitution of the country has placed it: in the hands of the Provinces.[4]

He ended with an apology for his "chilled answer."[5]

If Adelaide was disappointed with the response, she could at least draw some comfort from the realization that she had mentioned the matter to the prime minister. Perhaps the suggestion would work unconsciously, and result in who knows what good. Meanwhile, she was simply too busy to brood.

Early in 1910 she left Hamilton for another trip to the United States. This time, her travels took her to Milwaukee, where she spoke to the American Association for the Promotion of Industrial Education. The speech created sufficient interest for the *Spectator* , among other newspapers, to reprint it in total.

> It is so pointed and clear, and so strongly worked out in favor of a cause in which the women as well as the men of Canada should have a deep interest, that no apology is offered for its reproduction for the instruction and conversion, if need be, for readers of the Spectator.[6]

After emphasizing that she would not be discussing her topic "from the standpoint of the teacher of the theoretical home-maker,"[7] Adelaide set her audience at ease.

> When asked to take Miss Marshall's place this morning, I could not help feeling, that it was providential that you did not have another paper or address on the trade school, because really I am afraid you will have trade school indigestion before you get through. I hope it will not produce the usual effect of indigestion and make you pessimistic. Sometimes too much of a good thing is difficult to assimilate.[8]

When the laughter subsided, Adelaide gave the audience more information on her own favourite "good thing" — domestic science. First, she emphasized that trade schools could not be successful unless students were given excellent materials with which to work. Then she slipped into a repetition of one of her recurring themes.

> The home has been called the workshop for the making of men, and as we are discussing industries, trade, and occupations in general, I think that is a very good standpoint from which to consider this question. 90% of the female population will be engaged, at some time, in this great industry. One speaker said yesterday, "women take to this vocation instinctively." Do you run your factories or shops by instinct, or by system? What would you think of a manufacturer who would establish a large manufactory and run it by instinct?.... Another speaker emphasized the present specialization of girls in domestic arts rather than in trade training. That speaker has an exaggerated idea of the training given to girls in the schools. Two years ago one of your able women made the following statement, at a convention. "After investigating 90 representative domestic science centers in the United States, she pronounced 30% hopelessly bad—I hope this won't hurt — 50% fair and 20% so good as to illustrate the value of the subject when properly taught. Gentlemen, that is the condition of domestic science in your country. I know it to be true not only from my association with your educators, but from my own experience.[9]

Adelaide explained the source of the problem by stating that, early in the domestic science movement many women considered a few months training at a cooking school sufficient training for a teacher of domestic science. Fortunately, the situation was improving, she said, before launching into a description of domestic science courses in public schools. As usual, she emphasized that domestic sceince was not solely cooking, although cooking had been given great importance, and drew laughter from her audience when she said, "I think that it is one very clear evidence of man's hand in our education organization, because they have provided so very thoroughly for cooking lessons."[10]

Adelaide told the audience that by teaching domestic science the condition of homes could be improved, and linked this to her opening statement about the need for good materials in industrial training. In this case, human beings were the material of a better society, and she warned what would result from the absence of domestic science education: juvenile delinquency and a general lack of appreciation for quality.

Despite her belief in the importance of domestic science, Adelaide said, I do not wish to give you the impression that I would limit a girl to this one occupation of home-making. That would be absurd, as there are too many reasons why girls must engage, even though temporarily, in trade and wage earning occupations.[11]

She urged the predominantly male sudience to convince their wives to work towards domestic science education.

> I have faith enough in the men of America and Canada, to believe that if we women do our work conscientiously and thoroughly, they will support us. But we cannot expect them to think for us; we cannot expect them, with their pressing business worries, and all the other cares of life to think of all the details concerning the education of women; we must have the women themselves awaken the mothers to their responsibility in this direction.[12]

Paradoxically, while Adelaide could not support votes for women, she showed herself to be definitely in favour of women's involvement in public life, especially in areas affecting women and their families. While ostensibly advocating trade school courses for girls, she was in fact arguing for extended domestic science education. She told the audience that, "The trade school may be the only opportunity that many of these girls will have to acquire any knowledge of home-making."[13] Because of that, she pleaded with her audience "those of you who are contemplating establishing trade schools, to see that the domestic side, the home industries, are developed in proportion to the other trades."[14]

From this speech it is apparent that Adelaide's opinions had changed little over the years. She saw trade schools and other industrial training for girls as merely an additional means to spread the true gospel of domestic science education. Regardless of the lip service she paid to the idea of women having to work for a living, in Adelaide's mind all women would have to run homes, and this occupation would take up most of their time. Thus domestic science education for girls superseded all other requirements. It does not seem to have occurred to her that time spent learning domestic science was time away from industrial training, and the consequent lack of expertise would keep women out of better paying industrial jobs for decades. Despite Adelaide's repeated assurances that she understood the problems besetting women, she never seems to have realized that many women needed wages for survival, even after marriage.

Unlike the women of Adelaide's social milieu, there were no male protectors to shelter thousands of women from the economic realities of life. Out of necessity, many women would continue working even after marriage and motherhood, a fact which seems to have been entirely alien to Adelaide. In retrospect, it becomes obvious that, in emphasizing domestic science education, Adelaide did women wage earners a great disservice.

Nevertheless, Adelaide was not alone in her views. No matter what the reality of social and economic conditions, in the stereotypical family of 1910 the man was the breadwinner, the woman chatelaine and nurturer. Adelaide's support of the status quo, coupled with her efforts to raise woman's work to a profession, continued to charm vast numbers of those who listened to her or read the reports of her speeches. And she continued to be in demand as a guest speaker.

As well as speaking in Milwaukee, Adelaide travelled to New York for visits to various trade schools. While there she stayed at the Waldorf-Astoria Hotel and found time to write a letter home to Edna. After reassuring her daughter about her health, she described James Norris Oliphant who was about to become engaged to Muriel Hoodless.

James, who was a member of the stock exchange, had been Adelaide's escort on various outings in New York City. Apparently the Hoodless family had some misgivings about him, but now Adelaide was delighted to tell Edna,

> He is twice as nice when M is not around and does things in good style. He would give me the moon if I thought I wanted it.... But oh dear! He is terribly in love — it is really pitiable. He has got to the end of his endurance (*confidential*) and only an earthquake will keep him from Hamilton on Friday. I am seriously in fits. [15]

The note gives a rare glimpse into Adelaide's family life, showing how deeply interested in personal relationships she was, as well as her acute powers of observation and ability to be amused at human foibles.

Much to the young man's relief, his engagement to Muriel was announced on 15 February. A June wedding was planned. While Adelaide discussed arrangements for the event with her daughters, she continued to fulfill various speaking engagements. It is possible that her failing health, or sheer exhaustion, convinced her to cancel some of them. On 25 February, for instance, a 'causerie' was held under the auspices of the Women's Wentworth Historical Society. The guest speaker was George Creelman, who spoke on education and agriculture. Adelaide did not attend, although her name was brought up during the course of the evening. Creelman praised her highly, and his remarks were duly reported in the Hamilton newspapers.

The next day, Saturday, 26 February, Adelaide took the 12:25 train from Hamilton to Toronto. On board, she went over the notes of her speech one last time, adding a word here and there, deleting obscure or confusing sentences. At Union Station she walked briskly, sure of where she was going. She had been invited to speak at St. Margaret's College on Bloor Street East, and the topic of her discussion was Woman and Industrial Life.

The audience was largely made up of members of the Toronto Women's Canadian Club, and Adelaide easily captured their attention. Her expertise in the fields of domestic science and industrial education were widely accepted, regardless of various criticisms which emerged from time to time. Most of her listeners knew her by reputation as a woman of vision and boundless energy, a dedicated crusader who had turned dream after dream into reality. Even those who were not particularly interested in Adelaide's message were attracted by her open face, stately figure, and the warmth and wit of her speech.

About ten minutes into the talk, Adelaide's voice suddenly failed.

Unsteadily, she put her hand to her head as though in pain. A murmur of concern rippled through the audience. Mrs. R. A. Falconer, who was presiding over the meeting, rose from her chair behind Adelaide and handed her a glass of water. Adelaide smiled gratefully,sipped the water, and continued. "The interest in domestic —"[16] Suddenly the glass shattered on the floor as Adelaide collapsed.

Dr. Helen MacMurchie, an acquaintance of Adelaide, Dr. Julia Thomas, and two nurses rushed to her aid as the audience buzzed with concern. Someone sent for Dr. John Hunter, Adelaide's older brother, who lived in the city. By the time he reached the hall he could only confirm what the audience was already struggling to grasp: Adelaide Hoodless was dead of heart failure. There was nothing to do but telephone John, who, with his son-in-law Harry Bostwick, arrived by train a few hours later to take Adelaide's body home to Hamilton.

The papers broke the story on Monday. The *Hamilton Herald* made it front page news. Under the headline "Shocked by Sudden Death" was a picture of Adelaide in a light-coloured dress, her silvery hair caught up in a psyche knot. Two decades earlier, the newspapers had criticized Adelaide severely, deriding her as a faddist, a radical "new" woman. Now there was only praise. "Few women had a greater claim on the gratitude of the citizens of Hamilton than had Mrs. Hoodless,"[17] the *Herald* reported.

> Personally, Mrs. Hoodless was an amiable, cheerful and bright person. Although an enthusiast in matters of woman's welfare, she was well posted on all subjects of public moment; yet in her home and social life was a sweet, large-hearted, whole-souled woman, kind and thoughtful, and gathered around her a large circle of bright and happy people, among whom she was held in the highest regard.[18]

In the eulogies, the newspapers in Hamilton, Toronto, and other cities listed her many achievements.

> Mrs. Hoodless represented Canada at the International Congress of Women at London, England, where she was presented to the Late Queen Victoria; also at Washington, D. C. and at the meeting of Women's Clubs at St. Louis, Missouri. She was the founder of the Ontario Normal School of Domestic Arts in this city, and obtained from Sir William Macdonald of Montreal, the means with which Macdonald Institute at Guelph was erected. At the last meeting of the International Congress of Women she was appointed Chairman of the Technical Education section. For several years she had acted in an advisory capacity to the Department of Education, Ontario. She was recently appointed to the Advisory Committee of the Carnegie Institute, Pittsburgh, on Technical Education, and at the time of her decease was investigating the whole question of technical education and trade schools for girls. One of her last addresses, given at Milwaukee on this subject, caused widespread interest and comment in education centres in the United States, as well as in Canada.[19]

At 2:30 in the afternoon of Tuesday, 1 March, the funeral procession left Eastcourt for the Hamilton cemetary, where funeral services were conducted by Reverand Canon Wade. In addition to Adelaide's family, many friends and colleagues were present, including Hamilton's Mayor MacLaren and George Creelman, as well as representatives of various organizations with which Adelaide had been involved. Floral tributes bore silent witness to the love and respect Adelaide had inspired in her lifetime. There had been many messages of condolences, too, including a telegram from Governor-General Earl Grey:

> More shocked and grieved than I can say at the announcement of the sudden close of Mrs. Hoodless' splendid activities. Please accept from Lady Grey and myself our profound and heartfelt sympathy.[20]

Following the funeral, Adelaide's family and friends found some comfort in their memories and the fact that Adelaide's legacy was much more than their own fond reminiscences. In a career spanning just two decades, she had helped bring about many changes in Candian life. It was readily apparent that Adelaide's memory would survive, at least in Hamilton, Guelph, and Stoney Creek, where her contributions were well known. But none of her family could have dreamed as they struggled to accept their loss was that in time her legacy would reach out around the world, encompassing families who had never heard of Adelaide Hoodless, or Hamilton, or, for that matter, Canada.

Adelaide and John Hoodless, ca. 1905.

Epilogue

With Adelaide gone, her family coped as best they could. On 1 June, Muriel married James Oliphant in a quiet ceremony at the Church of the Ascension.

John Hoodless never remarried. A few weeks after Adelaide's death, he laid the cornerstone of the Adelaide Hunter Hoodless School, which was opened in November 1911. At the opening ceremonies, the *Spectator* reported, John "referred to the fact that within a stone's throw of what had been their happy home this memorial to his wife had been raised."[1] John lived quietly, still involved in Hamilton public life, until his death in January 1923. He did not survive long enough to see two more important buildings — the Adelaide Hoodless Homestead in St. George and the Erland Lee Home in Stoney Creek — dedicated to the memory of Adelaide and her contributions to Canadian life.

Edna Hoodless Bostwick followed her mother's example, and combined family responsibilities with public service. She and Harry had two children, James and Muriel, and when she was not caring for them, Edna was busy with duties at the Red Cross, the Victorian Order of Nurses, and the Local Council of women. Like Adelaide, Edna also enjoyed golf. In 1933, she won a provincial parent and child tournament with her son. She died in 1946.

Edna's son, James Montgomery Bostwick, was born at the end of the first world war. During the second, he served with distinction in Europe, where he was killed in action in 1944. He left behind a widow, Jean Soule whom he had married in 1941, but no children.

James' sister Muriel, named for her aunt, never married. Like her mother and grandmother, Muriel Bostwick was active in many Hamilton organizations. She worked as secretary to the city's Crown Attorney until shortly before her death in 1966. Her will bequeathed the Hoodless papers, on which this book is largely based, to the University of Guelph.

Adelaide's second child, Bernard, gave up his agricultural career to work alongside his father in the family furniture business. Like many patriotic Canadians, he volunteered for service as soon as World War I broke out in August 1914. Severely wounded in August 1918, he spent three years in hospital. After his recovery, he took up teaching at the Ontario Agricultural College in Guelph. He was still there when he died of a cerebral hemorrhage in April 1929, at the age of 44.

I have been unable to discover much information about Adelaide's third surviving child, Muriel. By the time of her brother's death, she had remarried, and was living with her husband, J. B. Peck, in Montreal. She was still alive in the mid-1950s. It seems Muriel did not have any children, and so Adelaide's line ended with the death of her granddaughter, Muriel Bostwick, in 1966.

If her family has disappeared, Adelaide's works provide some claim to immortality. Unfortunately, time has obscured many of her contributions. Her work with the YWCA and the Council of Women has been dimmed by the passing years and the number of equally dedicated women who have given their time and energy to these organizations. Her work in the field of domestic science has been depreciated because of the changes in educational and feminist ideologies. Ironically, it has been the Women's Institute, the organization which Adelaide founded but was only marginally involved with, which has done the most to preserve her memory.

During Adelaide's lifetime, the Women's Institute was basically a Canadian phenomenon. By June 1902, there were 39 Institutes, with 3081 members. The following year, when the first Institute convention was held at Macdonald Institute in Guelph, there were 4,500 members, and the organization continued to grow.

In 1910, the year of Adelaide's death, Madge Watt joined the Women's Institute in Metchosin on Vancouver Island. Mrs. Watt had been born Madge Robertson, near Collingwood, Ontario, in 1868. Graduating from the University of Toronto with a Master's degree in Arts, she worked at a New York newspaper until her marriage to Dr. Alfred Watt, a Canadian civil servant. When her husband was posted to William Head quarantine station on Vancouver Island, the Watts started a sheep farm.

After her husband's death in 1913, Madge took her two young sons to England in order to further their education. There, she proposed the idea of a Women's Institute, and easily won other women to her point of view.

> She was so charged with a bubbling vitality and contagious enthusiasm
> .... she had an ability to infect other people with her own enthusiasm
> which really did amount to genius.[2]

The Women's Institute also received royal sanction. Queen Mary heard of the organization and invited Madge to Sandringham to explain their operation. As a result of that interview, the Sandringham Women's Institute was established with the queen as president.

The Women's Institutes were established in Britain at a crucial time in that country's history. In 1915, England was at war and food was strictly rationed. As a result of the practice of the Women's Institute, the food supply was increased between 35% and 60%. Prime Minister Stanley Baldwin described the organization as ''the greatest idea that has come out of the colonies to the Motherland.''[3] For her work, Madge Watt received numerous honours, including an O.B.E. as well as the French *Medaille d'Agriculture*.

Nor did the Women's Institutes confine themselves to Britain. Gradually, they spread around the world, and, as the Associated Country of Women of the World, the organization continues its activities in such places as Australia, New Zealand, and Sri Lanka.

At the same time, the Canadian Institute has taken important steps to preserve its heritage. In Stoney Creek, the Erland Lee home has become a museum commemorating the site of the first Women's Institute in Canada. In St. George, Adelaide's birthplace has been restored and opened to the public. Both locations are visited yearly by hundreds of women from across the country and around the world.

The history of the Women's Institute has not been without its problems, however. In Canada, urbanization has taken its toll. The membership of the Federated Women's Institutes of Canada, the national body which unites Institutes across the country, is declining. Recently, members began to consider changes aimed at revitalizing the organization. The need for revitalization has become increasingly obvious for two reasons: the changing role of women in Canadian society and the economic crisis facing farm families. More than a century after Adelaide became involved in public life there is still the need for various reforms to help women and their families lead happier, more productive lives. The circumstances have changed, the terms applied to the problems and the solutions are different, but the need for women with imagination, dedication, and energy remains. It is a situation which Adelaide Sophia Hunter Hoodless would have understood.

Chronology

1857	27 February	Addie Hunter born, St. George, Ontario.
1881	14 September	Addie marries John Hoodless of Hamilton.
1882	7 July	Addie's first child, Edna Clarkson, born.
1884	10 December	Birth of Joeseph Bernard Hoodless.
1886	27 July	Birth of Muriel Adelaide Hoodless.
1888	23 July	Birth of John Harold Hoodless.
1889	18 March	Meeting to organize Hamilton YWCA.
	20 May	Hamilton YWCA residence opens.
	10 August	Death of John Harold Hoodless.
1890	September	Adelaide becomes 2nd president of YWCA.
1893	May	Adelaide attends International Congress of Women at Chicago World's Fair.
	27 October	Inaugural meeting of National Council of Women, Toronto. Adelaide elected treasurer.
	17 November	Inaugural meeting of Hamilton Local Council.
1894	20 January	Cooking classes open under the auspices of the Hamilton YWCA.
	11 April	First convention of the National Council of Women of Canada opens.
	12 April	Adelaide reads papers on domestic science and urges Local Councils to work towards the establishment of courses in public schools.
	July	Adelaide approaches Hamilton Board of Education with request to introduce domestic science.
	September	School of Domestic Science, under auspices of Hamilton YWCA, opens.
1895	23 January	Adelaide elected president of Dominion YWCA.
1896	December	Adelaide's speech at Ontario Agricultural College brings invitation from Erland Lee to speak at Farmer's Institute Ladies' Night.
1897	January	Ontario provincial government introduces legislation allowing for the inclusion of domestic science courses in public schools.

		Hamilton Board of Education accepts YWCA offer to teach domestic science to selected public school students.
		Around this time, Adelaide begins work as domestic science publicist for Department of Education.
	12 February	Adelaide suggests formation of an organization for rural women at Farmer's Institute Ladies' Night, Stoney Creek.
	19 February	Adelaide addresses inaugural meeting of Women's Institute.
	25 February	First formal meeting of the Women's Institute. Adelaide named honourary president.
1898		Publication of *Public School Domestic Science* , Adelaide's textbook.
	6 January	Hamilton Board of Education voters to end arrangement with YWCA for teaching of domestic science to public school pupils.
	October	Kingston YWCA opens domestic science school similar to Hamilton's.
1899	8 March	Meeting of the executive of the VON, Hamilton, including Adelaide. Plans formulated to bring VON nurse to the city.
	10 March	Adelaide completes report on Domestic Science for Department of Education.
	June-July	Adelaide in Britain for International Council of Women conference.
1900	1 February	Ontario Normal School of Domestic Science and Art, Hamilton, opens, with Adelaide as president.
	9 March	Hamilton Board of Education again votes to allow students to attend domestic science courses, at ONSDSA.
1901	17 April	Adelaide resigns from National Council of Women.
	23 October	Adelaide visits Montreal, speaks to Sir William Macdonald on Guelph project, and reports optimistically on results.
		John Hoodless' business in financial trouble: assignee appointed.
1902	2 January	Richard Harcourt congratulates Adelaide on her part in convincing Sir William Macdonald to support Guelph scheme.

	30 September	Adelaide resigns presidency of the Hamilton YWCA.
	9 October	Richard Harcourt writes to Hamilton Board of Education urging immediate establishment of domestic science classes.
	13 November	Hamilton Board of Education begins process leading to establishment of domestic science classes in its public schools.
		Adelaide's first nervous breakdown occurred around this time.
1903	13 January	Adelaide storms out of Hamilton YWCA meeting after being overlooked as member of Board of Directors.
		By end of year, classes being held in Guelph, although Macdonald Institute building yet to be completed.
1904	August	Adelaide's courses at Guelph cancelled.
	7 December	Formal opening of Macdonald Institute. Adelaide among the speakers.
1905		Early in the year, Adelaide's second nervous breakdown occurred.
1907	9 October	Edna Hoodless marries Harry Bostwick.
1908		Adelaide resigns from National Council position as provincial vice-president and convenor of Domestic Science Committee.
		Adelaide begins to investigate industrial education for girls for the Department of Education.
1909	March	Adelaide made advisor to Carnegie Technical schools, Pittsburgh.
1910	February	Adelaide addresses American Association for the Promotion of Industrial Education, Milwaukee.
	15 February	Muriel Hoodless's engagement to James Oliphant announced.
	26 February	Adelaide Hunter Hoodless dies in Toronto.
	1 March	Adelaide buried in Hamilton.

Notes

Chapter One
[1] Ruth Howes, *Adelaide Hoodless, Woman with a Vision* . (Millett, Alberta: 1965), p. 17.
[2] *Toronto Globe and Mail*, 28 February 1910.
[3] *Muriel Bostwick to Ruth Howes*, 17 February 1966, in Hoodless Family Papers.
[4] *History of Ontario* in Hoodless Family Papers.
[5] Hoodless Family Papers.
[6] Hoodless Family Papers.
[7] Howes, p. 15.
[8] Michael B. Katz, *People of Hamilton, Canada West: Family and Class in a Mid-Nineteenth Century City* (Cambridge: 1975), p. xv.
[9] *The Hamilton Spectator*, 30 January 1889.
[10] *The Hamilton Spectator*, 10 August 1889.

Chapter Two
[1] May Harrington Farmer, *One Hundred Years: The Church of the Ascension, A Short History 1850-1950* (Hamilton: 1950), p. 15.
[2] Mary Quaylle Innis, *Unfold the Years: A History of the Young Women's Christian Association in Canada* . (Toronto: 1949)
[3] Innis, *Unfold the Years*
[4] *The Hamilton Spectator*, 26 May 1893.
[5] *The Hamilton Spectator*, 26 May 1893.
[6] Address by Edna Hoodless Bostwick in Hoodless Family Papers.
[7] *The Hamilton Spectator*, 30 January 1889.
[8] *Hamilton Evening Times, 27 January 1892.*
[9] Innis, *Unfold the Years*, p. 27.
[10] *Hamilton Evening Times* , 11 April 1892.

Chapter Three
[1] *The Hamilton Spectator* , 3 May 1893.
[2] May Wright Sewall, *World's Congress of Representative Women, A Historical Resumé* (Chicago: 1894), p. 31.
[3] Sewall, p. 110.
[4] Sewall, p. 361.
[5] *Hamilton Times* ca. November 1893, in Hoodless Family Papers.
[6] Hoodless Family Papers.
[7] Ishbel Aberdeen, *We, Twa* (London: 1925) p. 295.
[8] Aberdeen, p. 295.
[9] Aberdeen, p. 296.
[10] *The Globe and Mail*, 28 October 1893.
[11] *The Globe* , 28 October 1893.
[12] *The Globe* , 28 October 1893.
[13] *The Globe* , 28 October 1893.
[14] *The Globe* , 28 October 1893.
[15] *The Globe* , 28 October 1893.
[16] *the Globe* , 28 October 1893.
[17] *The Globe* , 28 October 1893.
[18] *The Globe* , 28 October 1893.
[19] *Twenty-Six Years of Activity of the Hamilton Local Council of Women, 1893-1919. (Hamilton: 1920).*
[20] Newspaper report, 28 October 1904 in Hoodless Family Papers.
[21] Aberdeen, p. 300.
[22] Mary Quayle Innis, *The Clear Spirit: Twenty Canadian Women and Their Times* (Toronto: University of Toronto Press, 1965) p. 111.
[23] Innis, *The Clear Spirit* pp. 110-111.
[24] *Hamilton Evening Times* , 18 November 1893.

[25] *Hamilton Evening Times* , 18 November 1893.
[26] *Hamilton evening Times* , ca November 1893 in Hoodless Family Papers.

Chapter Four
[1] *Hamilton Evening Times* , 22 January 1894.
[2] Shirley F. Murphy, *Our Homes and How to Make Them Healthy*, quoted in *The Light of the Home* . p. 312.
[3] M. M. Cornelius, *The Young Housekeeper's Friend*, Boston, quoted in *The Light of the Home* , (Boston: 1868), p. 9.
[4] M. M. Cornelius, p. 135.
[5] M. M. Cornelius, p. 135.
[6] M. M. Cornelius, pp. 135-136.
[7] *The Hamilton Spectator* , 6 February 1889.
[8] Hoodless Family Papers.
[9] Innis, *The Clear Spirit* , p. 111.
[10] Hoodless Family Papers.
[11] Gardiner Scrapbooks, Vol. 277, p. 93.
[12] Gardiner Scrapbooks, p. 93.
[13] Speech made in Milwaukee, February, 1910 in Hoodless Family Papers.
[14] British Columbia Women's Institutes, *Modern Pioneers* (Evergreen Press Limited) p. 5.
[15] *Modern Pioneers* , p. 5.
[16] Hoodless Family Papers.
[17] Newspaper report, 13 March 1894 in Hoodless Family Papers.
[18] Newspaper report, 13 March 1894 in Hoodless Family Papers.
[19] Newspaper report, 13 March 1894 in Hoodless Family Papers.
[20] *The Hamilton Spectator,* 13 March 1894.

Chapter Five
[1] *The Hamilton Spectator* .
[2] Newspaper report, 13 April 1894 in Hoodless Family Papers.
[3] Newspaper report, 13 April 1894 in Hoodless Family Papers.
[4] Newspaper report, 13 April 1894 in Hoodless Family Papers.
[5] Newspaper report, 13 April 1894 in Hoodless Family Papers.
[6] Newspaper report, 13 April 1894 in Hoodless Family Papers.
[7] Newspaper report, 13 April 1894 in Hoodless Family Papers.
[8] Newspaper report, 13 April 1894 in Hoodless Family Papers.
[9] *Hamilton Evening Times* , May 1894.
[10] *Hamilton Evening Times,* May 1894.
[11] *Hamilton Evening Times,* May 1894.
[12] Newspaper report, 13 July 1894 in Hoodless Family Papers.
[13] Newspaper report, 13 July 1894 in Hoodless Family Papers
[14] Newspaper report, 13 July 1894 in Hoodless Family Papers.
[15] Hamilton Local Council of Women *Twenty-Six Years of Activity of the Hamilton Local Council of Women, 1893-1919* (Hamilton: Spectator Print Shop, 1920)
[16] Edith Child Rowles, *Home Economics in Canada, The Early History of Six College Programs: Prologue to Change* (Saskatoon: Modern Press).
[17] *The Hamilton Spectator,* 22 September 1894.
[18] *Light of the Home* , p. 83
[19] It The Hamilton Spectator, 26 September 1894.
[20] *The Hamilton Spectator* , 11 October 1894.

Chapter Six
[1] Ishbel Aberdeen, *The Canadian Journals of Lady Aberdeen* (J. T. Saywell, ed.) 1960, p. 207.
[2] Ishbel Aberdeen, p. 208.
[3] *Hamilton Evening Times* , 21 September 1895.
[4] Newspaper report in Hoodless Family Papers.
[5] Newspaper report in Hoodless Family Papers.
[6] *The Hamilton Spectator* , 31 March 1896.
[7] *The Hamilton Spectator* , 31 March 1896.

[8] Hamilton Board of Education, *Minutes of the Hamilton Board of Education*, 1896.
[9] Minutes of the Hamilton Board of Education, 1896.
[10] *Minutes of the Hamilton Board of Education*, 1896.
[11] *Minutes of the Hamilton Board of Education*, 1896
[12] Newspaper report in Hoodless Family Papers.
[13] *The Hamilton Spectator*, 15 August 1896.
[14] Newspaper report in Hoodless Family Papers
[15] Hoodless Family Papers.
[16] *London Free Press*, 22 September 1896 in Hoodless Family Papers.
[17] *London Free Press*, 3 October 1896 in Hoodless Family Papers.
[18] *London Free Press*, 3 October 1896 in Hoodless Family Papers.

Chapter Seven

[1] *The Hamilton Spectator*, 9 October 1896.
[2] *The Hamilton Spectator*, October 1896 in Hoodless Family Papers.
[3] *The Hamilton Spectator*, October 1896 in Hoodless Family Papers.
[4] *The Hamilton Herald*, October 1896 in Hoodless Family Papers.
[5] *The Hamilton Herald*, October 1896 in Hoodless Family Papers.
[6] *Minutes of the Hamilton Board of Education* 1896.
[7] *The Hamilton Spectator*, 30 December 1896.
[8] Hoodless Family Papers.
[9] Hoodless Family Papers.
[10] Hoodless Family Papers.

Chapter Eight

[1] Hoodless Family Papers.
[2] Howes, p. 12.
[3] *Modern Pioneers*, p. 11.
[4] *The Clear Spirit*, p. 114.
[5] *Home Economics in Canada*, p. 38.
[6] *Home Economics in Canada*, p. 38.
[7] *Modern Pioneers*, p. 13.

Chapter Nine

[1] *Hamilton Times*, 30 June 1897.
[2] *Hamilton Times*, 30 June 1897.
[3] *Hamilton Times*, 30 June 1897.
[4] *The Hamilton Spectator* editorial ca. 1897 in Hoodless Family Papers.
[5] *Brantford Exposition* in Hoodless Family Papers.
[6] Adelaide Hoodless, *Public School Domestic Science* (Toronto: Copp Clark, 1898) p. vi.
[7] Adelaide Hoodless, p. ix.
[8] Adelaide Hoodless, p. 16.
[9] Adelaide Hoodless, p. 196.
[10] Adelaide Hoodless, p. x.
[11] Adelaide Hoodless, pp. 104-105.
[12] Adelaide Hoodless, p. 160.
[13] Adelaide Hoodless, pp. 128-129.
[14] Twenty-Six Years, pp. 34-35.

Chapter Ten

[1] *Hamilton Times*, 7 January 1898.
[2] *Hamilton Times*, 8 January 1898.
[3] *Hamilton Times*, 8 January 1898.
[4] *Hamilton Times*, 8 January 1898.
[5] Hamilton newspaper in Hoodless Family Papers.
[6] Hamilton newspaper in Hoodless Family Papers.
[7] *Toronto Globe*, 20 May 1898.
[8] *Hamilton Times, 18 July 1898*.
[9] *Minutes of the Hamilton Board of Education, 1898, p. 77*.
[10] Kingston newspaper ca. 30 October 1898 in Hoodless Family Papers.

[11] Letter dates 6 October 1898 in Hoodless Family Papers.
[12] *Canadian Who Was Who, 1875-1933: A Standard Dictionary of Canadian Biography* (Toronto: 1934).
[13] *Brantford Expositor*, 1898 in Hoodless Family Papers.
[14] *London Free Press*, 1897 in Hoodless Family Papers.
[15] *Brantford Expositor*, 1898 in Hoodless Family Papers.
[16] Orangeville newspaper ca. December 1908 in Hoodless Family Papers.
[17] Belleville newspaper, ca. 15 March 1902 in Hoodless Family Papers.
[18] *Saint John Globe*, 1902 in Hoodless Family Papers.
[19] *Ottawa Free Press*, October 1902 in Hoodless Family Papers.
[20] *Ottawa Free Press*, October 1902 in Hoodless Family Papers.
[21] *Berlin News Record*, 28 February 1902 inHoodless Family Papers.
[22] *Canadian Who Was Who* .
[23] newspaper report 7 December 1904 in Hoodless Family Papers.
[24] *Pittsburgh Gazette* 16 October 1908 in Hoodless Family Papers.
[25] Women Workers of Canada, 1899.
[26] Cleveland newspaper, October 1908 in Hoodless Family Papers.
[27] *Hamilton Herald*, 18 February 1902.
[28] *Hamilton Herald*, 18 February 1902.
[29] Innis, *The Clear Spirit*, p. 112.
[30] Letter from Hoodless to Harcourt, 13 March 1902 in Ontario Archives.
[31] Hoodless to Harcourt, 15 March 1902.
[32] Hoodless to Harcourt, 23 Octopber 1902.
[33] Hoodless to Harcourt, 23 October 1902.
[34] Letter from Harcourt to Hoodless, 22 October 1902 in Ontario Archives.
[35] Letter from Hoodless to Harcourt, 29 October 1902 in Ontario Archives.
[36] Newspaper report, 1904 in Hoodless Family Papers.
[37] Newspaper report, 1904 in Hoodless Family Papers.
[38] Hoodless Family Papers.

Chapter Eleven
[1] Adelaide Hoodless, *Report of Mrs. Hoodless on Domestic Science* .
[2] *London Free Press*, 4 March 1899.
[3] *London Free Press*, 4 March 1899.
[4] *London Free Press*, 4 March 1899.
[5] *London Free Press*, 4 March 1899.
[6] *London Free Press*, 8 March 1899.
[7] *London Free Press*, 8 March 1899.
[8] *London Free Press*, 10 March 1899.
[9] *London Free Press*, 10 March 1899.
[10] *London Free Press*, 11 March 1899.
[11] *London Free Press*, 16 March 1899.
[12] *Minutes of the Hamilton Board of Education*, 1899, p. 47.
[13] Letter from Charles Tupper to Adelaide Hoodless, 9 March 1899 in Hoodless Family Papers.
[14] *Toronto Mail & Empire*, report filed 22 June 1899 in Hoodless Family Papers.
[15] *Toronto Mail & Empire*, report filed 22 June 1899 in Hoodless Family Papers.
[16] *Toronto Mail & Empire*, report filed 22 June 1899 in Hoodless Family Papers.
[17] *Toronto Mail & Empire*, report filed 22 June 1899 in Hoodless Family Papers.
[18] *Toronto Mail & Empire*, report filed 27 June 1899 in Hoodless Family Papers.
[19] *Toronto Mail & Empire*, report filed 27 June 1899 in Hoodless Family Papers.
[20] *Toronto Mail & Empire*, report filed 27 June 1899 in Hoodless Family Papers.
[21] *Toronto Mail & Empire*, report filed 27 June 1899 in Hoodless Family Papers.
[22] *Toronto Mail & Empire*, report filed 8 July 1899 in Hoodless Family Papers.
[23] *Toronto Mail & Empire*, report filed 8 July 1899 in Hoodless Family Papers.
[24] *Toronto Mail & Empire*, report filed 1 July 1899 in Hoodless Family Papers.
[25] *Toronto Mail & Empire*, report filed 20 July 1899 in Hoodless Family Papers.
[26] *Toronto Mail & Empire*, report filed 22 July 1899 in Hoodless Family Papers.
[27] *Toronto Mail & Empire*, report filed 22 July 1899 in Hoodless Family Papers.
[28] *Toronto Mail & Empire*, report filed 22 July 1899 in Hoodless Family Papers.

[29] *Toronto Mail & Empire*, report filed 22 July 1899 in Hoodless Family Papers.
[30] *Toronto Mail & Empire*, report filed 22 July 1899 in Hoodless Family Papers.
[31] *Toronto Mail & Empire*, report filed 22 July 1899 in Hoodless Family Papers.
[32] *Toronto Mail & Empire*, report filed 20 July 1899 in Hoodless Family Papers.
[33] *Toronto Mail & Empire*, report filed 20 July 1899 in Hoodless Family Papers.
[34] *Toronto Mail & Empire*, report filed 20 July 1899 in Hoodless Family Papers.

Chapter Twelve
[1] report in *The Philadelphia Record*, 1899 in Hoodless Family Papers.
[2] report in *The Philadelphia Record*, 1899 in Hoodless Family Papers.
[3] *Hamilton Herald*, 1899.
[4] *Toronto World*, January 1900 in Hoodless Family Papers.
[5] *Toronto World*, January 1900 in Hoodless Family Papers.
[6] *Toronto World*, January 1900 in Hoodless Family Papers.
[7] *Hamilton evening Times*, 2 February 1900.
[8] *The Hamilton Herald* 2 February 1900.
[9] *The Hamilton Spectator*, 2 February 1900.
[10] *Hamilton Evening Times*, 2 February 1900.
[11] *Hamilton Evening Times*, 2 February 1900.
[12] *Hamilton Evening Times, 9 March 1900.*
[13] *Toronto Daily Star*, 3 October 1900.
[14] *Toronto Daily Star, 3 October 1900.*
[15] Letter from Adelaide Hoodless to Richard Harcourt, 15 July 1901 in Ontario Archives.
[16] *Hamilton Evening Times*, 17 December 1901.
[17] *Minutes of the Hamilton Board of Education*, 1901.
[18] *The Hamilton Spectator*, 1 October 1902.

Chapter Thirteen
[1] Undated letter in Hoodless Family Papers.
[2] Letter from James Mills to Adelaide Hoodless, 9 March 1900 in Hoodless Family Papers.
[3] *Into the Twentieth Century*, p. 5.
[4] *Into the Twentieth Century*, p. 5.
[5] Letter from William Macdonald to Lady Minto, 12 April 1900 in Hoodless Family Papers.
[6] Letter to Sir William Macdonald, 8 March 1901 in Hoodless Family Papers.
[7] Letter to Sir William Macdonald, 8 March 1901 in Hoodless Family Papers.
[8] Letter from Adelaide Hoodless to Richard Harcourt,15 October 1901 in Ontario Archives.
[9] Letter from Adelaide Hoodless to Richard Harcourt, 15 October 1901 in Ontario Archives.
[10] Hoodless Family Papers.
[11] Letter from Adelaide Hoodless to Richard Harcourt, 23 October 1901 in Ontario Archives.

Chapter Fourteen
[1] Letter from Harcourt to Hoodless, 2 January 1902 in Ontario Archives.
[2] Letter from Hoodless to Harcourt, 8 January 1902 in Ontario Archives.
[3] Hoodless to Harcourt, 10 January 1902.
[4] Hoodless to Harcourt, 15 January 1902.
[5] Hoodless to Harcourt, 5 August 1901.
[6] Hoodless to Harcourt, 5 August 1901.
[7] Hoodless to Harcourt, 5 August 1901.
[8] Hoodless to Harcourt, 26 November 1901.
[9] Hoodless to Harcourt, 1 March 1904.
[10] Adelaide Hoodless, Report: *YWCA & Technical Institute* Hamilton, 17 January 1902.
[11] Letter from William C. Macdonald to J. Robertson, 13 February 1902 in Hoodless Family Papers.
[12] Typewritten copy of an Order-in-Council in Hoodless Family Papers.
[13] Letter from Adelaide Hoodless to Richard Harcourt, 23 April 1902 in Ontairo Archives.
[14] Letter from James Mills to Adelaide Hoodless, 10 May 1902 in Hoodless Family Papers.
[15] Letter from Adelaide Hoodless to Richard Harcourt, 5 May 1902 in Ontario Archives.
[16] Hoodless to Harcourt, 30 May 1902.
[17] Hoodless to Harcourt, 30 May 1902.

[18] Hoodless to Harcourt,19 July 1902.
[19] Letter from Richard Harcourt to Adelaide Hoodless, 18 September 1902 in Ontario Archives.
[20] *The Hamilton Spectator,* 1 October 1902.
[21] *Mail & Empire,* 11 October 1902.
[22] Letter from Adelaide Hoodless to Richard Harcourt, 11 October 1902 in Ontario Archives.

Chapter Fifteen
[1] Letter from Adelaide Hoodless to Richard Harcourt, 29 October 1902 in Ontario Archives.
[2] Letter from Richard Harcourt to Adelaide Hoodless, 31 October 1902 in Ontario Archives.
[3] Harcourt to Hoodless, 31 October 1902.
[4] Harcourt to Hoodless, 31 October 1902.
[5] Harcourt to Hoodless, 31 October 1902.
[6] Harcourt to Hoodless, 31 October 1902.
[7] Harcourt to Hoodless, 31 October 1902.
[8] Harcourt to Hoodless, 31 October 1902.
[9] Harcourt to Hoodless, 31 October 1902.
[10] Harcourt to Hoodless, 20 November 1902.
[11] Letter from Adelaide Hoodless to Richard Harcourt, 22 November 1902 in Ontario Archives.
[12] Hoodless to Harcourt, 16 December 1902.
[13] Hoodless to Harcourt, 16 December 1902.
[14] Hoodless to Harcourt, 16 December 1902.
[15] Hoodless to Harcourt, 16 December 1902.
[16] Hoodless to Harcourt, 16 December 1902.
[17] *Hamilton Evening Times,* 14 January 1903.
[18] *Hamilton Evening Times,* 14 January 1903.
[19] *The Hamilton Spectator,* 14 January 1903.
[20] *Hamilton Evening Times,* 14 January 1903.
[21] *Hamilton Evening Times,* 14 January 1903.
[22] *Hamilton Evening Times,* 14 January 1903.
[23] *The Hamilton Herald,* 16 January 1903 in Hoodless Family Papers.
[24] *The Hamilton Herald,* 16 January 1903 in Hoodless Family Papers.
[25] Letter form Richard Harcourt to Adelaide Hoodless, 26 January 1903 in Ontario Archives.
[26] Letter from Adelaide Hoodless to Richard Harcourt, 6 February 1903 in Ontario Archives.
[27] Hoodless to Harcourt, 6 February 1903.
[28] Hoodless to Harcourt, 6 February 1903.
[29] Letter from Richard Harcourt to Adelaide Hoodless, 9 February 1903 in Ontario Archives.
[30] Harcourt to Hoodless, 9 February 1903.
[31] Harcourt to Hoodless, 29 October 1902.
[32] Harcourt to Hoodless, 6 February 1903.
[33] *The Hamilton Spectator,* 15 May 1903.
[34] *The Hamilton Spectator,* 15 May 1903.
[35] Letter from Adeliade Hoodless to Richard Harcourt, 8 June 1903 in Ontario Archives.

Chapter Sixteen
[1] Letter from James Mills to Adelaide Hoodless, 5 October 1903 in Hoodless Family Papers.
[2] Mills to Hoodless, 5 October 1903.
[3] Mills to Hoodless, 5 October 1903.
[4] Provincial Announcement re: Macdonald Institute, August 1903 in Hoodless Family Papers.
[5] Hoodless Family Papers.
[6] Hoodless Family Papers.
[7] Hoodless Family Papers.
[8] "A Farm Home" in *East and West,* 28 March 1908, p. 101 in Hoodless Family Papers.
[9] Introduction to Ethics and the Home in Hoodless Family Papers.
[10] Letter from Adelaide Hoodless to Richard Harcourt, 9 January 1904 in Ontario Archives.
[11] Hoodless to Harcourt, 9 January 1904.
[12] Hoodless to Harcourt, 9 January 1904.
[13] Hoodless to Harcourt, 9 January 1904.

[14] Alice Ravenill, quoted by Terence Crowley in "Madonnas before Magdelenes: Adelaide Hoodless and the Making of the Canadian Gibson Girl." (manuscript)
[15] Letter from George Creelman to Adelaide Hoodless, 19 February 1904 in Hoodless Family Papers.
[16] Hoodless Family Papers, 18 August 1904.
[17] Hoodless Family Papers, 18 August 1904.
[18] Hoodless Family Papers, 18 August 1904.
[19] Hoodless Family Papers, 18 August 1904.
[20] Hoodless Family Papers, 18 August 1904.
[21] Hoodless Family Papers, 18 August 1904.
[22] Newspaper report, 7 December 1904 in Hoodless Family Papers.

Chapter Seventeen
[1] Letter from Adelaide Hoodless to Richard Harcourt, 22 April 1904 in Ontario Archives.
[2] *Hamilton Evening Times*, 9 October 1907.
[3] *The Hamilton Spectator*, 10 October 1907.
[4] *The Hamilton Spectator*, 10 October 1907.
[5] Adelaide Hoodless, *Home Economics Report — given to the Domestic Education Association*, Toronto, 12 July 1907 in Hoodless Family Papers.
[6] Home Economics Report.
[7] Undated newspaper report in Hoodless Family Papers.
[8] *Hamilton Times*, May 1908.
[9] *Hamilton Times*, May 1908.
[10] *Hamilton Times*, May 1908.
[11] *London Free Times* (undated) in Hoodless Family Papers.
[12] Hoodless Family Papers.
[13] *Pittsburgh Gazette*, 16 October 1908 in Hoodless Family Papers.
[14] Adelaide Hoodless, *Report to the Minister of Education, Ontario, on Training Schools in Relation to Elementary Education* (Toronto: King's Printer, 1909) p. 4.
[15] Adelaide Hoodless, *Report to the Minister of Education...*, p. 14.
[16] Adelaide Hoodless, *Report to the Minister of Education...* .
[17] Adelaide Hoodless, *Report to the Minister of Education...*, p. 4.
[18] Adelaide Hoodless, *Report to the Minister of Education...*, p. 3.
[19] Adelaide Hoodless, *Report to the Minister of Education...*, p. 4.
[20] Adelaide Hoodless, *Report to the Minister of Education...*, p. 5.
[21] *The Hamilton Spectator*, 13 March 1909.
[22] *The Hamilton Herald*, 15 March 1909.

Chapter Eighteen
[1] Letter from Adelaide Hoodless to Sir Wilfred Laurier, 3 November 1909 in Hoodless Family Papers.
[2] Hoodless to Laurier, 3 November 1909.
[3] Letter from Sir Wilfred Laurier to Adelaide Hoodless, 6 November 1909 in Public Archives of Canada.
[4] Laurier to Hoodless, 6 November 1909.
[5] Laurier to Hoodless, 6 November 1909.
[6] *The Hamilton Spectator*, 12 February 1909.
[7] Transcript of Milwaukee Speech, January 1909 in Hoodless Family Papers.
[8] Milwaukee Speech, January 1909.
[9] Milwaukee Speech, January 1909.
[10] Milwaukee Speech, January 1909.
[11] Milwaukee Speech, January 1909.
[12] Milwaukee Speech, January 1909.
[13] Milwaukee Speech, January 1909.
[14] Milwaukee Speech, January 1909.
[15] Letter from Adelaide Hoodless to Edna Bostwick, 26 January 1910 in Hoodless Family Papers.
[16] *Toronto Sunday World*, 27 February 1910 in Hoodless Family Papers.
[17] *The Hamilton Herald*, 28 February 1910.
[18] *The Hamilton Herald*, 28 February 1910.

[19] *The Hamilton Herald*, 28 February 1910.
[20] *The Hamilton Herald*, 28 February 1910.

Epilogue
[1] *The Hamilton Spectator,* 2 November 1911.
[2] *Modern Pioneers*, p. 27.
[3] *Modern Pioneers*, p. 27.

General Bibliography

Aberdeen, Lady Ishbel. *We Twa* . London : 1925.

Bannerman, Jean. *Leading Ladies* . Belleville: Mika Publishing Company, 1977.

British Columbia Women's Institutes. *Modern Pioneers*. Evergreen Press Limited.

The Canadian Encyclopedia . Edmonton: Hurtig Publishers, 1985.

Canadian Who Was Who, 1875-1933: A Standard Dictionary of Canadian Biography . Toronto: 1934.

Dalley, Norman D. *A History of the Hamilton Branch of the Victorian Order of Nurses for Canada*. Hamilton: November 1966.

Duff, Frances I. *Highlights of the Hamilton YWCA 1889-1964*. Hamilton: 1964.

Farmer, May Harrington. *The Church of the Ascension, Hamilton: A Short History, 1850-1950* . Hamilton: Kidner Printing Company, May 1950.

Federated Women's Institutes of Ontario. *Erland Lee (Museum) Home* . May 1984.

Federated Women's Institutes of Ontario. *Ontario Women's Institute Story*, 1972.

Gibbon, John Murray. *Three Centuries of Canadian Nursing* . Toronto: Macmillan of Canada, 1947.

Gibbon, John Murray. *The Victorian Order of Nurses for Canada, Fiftieth Anniversary, 1897-1947* . Victorian Order of Nurses: 1947.

Hamilton Board of Education. *Minutes of the Proceedings of the Board of Education of the City of Hamilton* . Hamilton: Hamilton Times Printing Company, 1894-1910 (17 volumes).

Hamilton Local Council of Women. *Twenty-Six Years of Activity of the Hamilton Local Council of Women, 1893-1919* . Hamilton: Spectator Print Shop, 1920.

Harshaw, Josephine Perfect. *When Women Work together — A History of the YWCA of Canada 1870-1966*. Toronto: Ryerson Press, 1966.

Hodgins, J. George. *The Establishment of Schools and Colleges in Ontario 1792-1910* . Toronto: L. K. Cameron, King's Printing 1910.

Hoodless, Adelaide. *Home Economics* . Toronto: Dominion Education Association, July 1907.

Hoodless, Adelaide. *Public School Domestic Science*

Toronto: The Copp Clark Company Limited, 1898.

Hoodless, Adelaide. *Report to the Minister of Education, Ontario, on Trade Schools in Relation to Elementary Education* . Toronto: L. K. Cameron, King's Printer, 1909.

Howes, Ruth. *Adelaide Hoodless: Woman with a Vision* . Federated Women's Institutes of Canada, 1965.

Illustrated Historical Atlas of the County of Wentworth . Toronto: Page and Smith, 1875.

Innis, Mary Quayle, ed. *The Clear Spirit: Twenty Canadian Women and Their Times* . Toronto: University of Toronto Press, 1966.

Innis, Mary Quayle. *Unfold the Years: A History of the Young Women's Christian Association in Canada* . Toronto: McClelland & Stewart Limited, 1949.

International Council of Women. ''Who's Who at the Congress of Women''. (souvenir pamphlet) 1909.

Jeffries, B. G. and Nichols, J. L. *Searchlights on Health* . Toronto: J. L. Nichols Co. Ltd., 1894.

Johnson, Stanley. *A History of Emigration from the United Kingdom to North America, 1763-1912* . London: George Routledge & Songs Limited, 1913.

Katz, Michael B. *The People of Hamilton, Canada West: Family and Class in a Mid-Nineteenth Century City* . Cambridge: Harvard University Press, 1975.

National Council of Women of Canada. *Women of Canada, their Life and Work* . 1900.

Reville, F. Douglas. *History of the County of Brant* . Brantford: The Hurley Printing Co. Ltd., 1920.

Rich, Theodore D. *Hamilton, the Birmingham of Canada* . 1892.

Rowles, Edith child. *Home Economics in Canada, The Early History of Six College Programs: Prologue to Change* . Saskatoon: Modern Press.

Saywell, J. T., ed. *The Canadian Journals of Lady Aberdeen* . Ottawa: 1960.

Sewall, Mary Wright, ed. *The World's Congress of Representative Women* . Chicago: Rand McNally & Company, 1984 (2 volumes).

Shaw, Rosa L. *Proud Heritage: A History of the National Council of Women of Canada* . Toronto: The Ryerson Press, 1957.

Urquhart, M. C., ed. *Historical Statistics of Canada* . Toronto: Cambridge University Press, 1965.

Worcester, Alfred A. M. M.D. *Nurses and Training* . Cambridge: Harvard University Press, 1927.

Young Women's Christian Association of Hamilton. *A Centre for Girls* . Hamilton: 1929.

Newspapers

Berlin News Record	28 February 1902
Brant Expositor	1898
The Christian Guardian	10 October 1900
The Globe & Mail (Toronto)	25 October 1893
	28 May 1898
	28 February 1910
Hamilton Evening Times	1892-1898
	1900-1901
	1903
	1907
	1908
	1910
The Hamilton Herald	1899
	1902-1903
	1909-1910
The Hamilton Spectator	1890-1910
London Free Press	September-October 1896
	4-16 March 1899
Ottawa Free Press	October 1902
Philadelphia Record	1899
Pittsburgh Gazette	16 October 1902
	15 October 1908
Saint John Globe	1902
Toronto Daily Star	3 October 1900
Toronto Mail & Empire	June-July 1899
Toronto Sunday World	27 February 1910.
Toronto World	3 January 1900

Unpublished Sources

Hoodless Family Papers. Archival Collections, University of Guelph Library. (includes correspondence, phototgraphs, and hundreds of newspaper clippings.)

Ontario Archives. Correspondence between Richard Harcourt, Minister of Education and Adelaide Hoodless.

Public Archives of Canada. Correspondence between Adelaide Hoodless and Sir Wilfred Laurier.

Hamilton Public Library, Special Collections: Gardiner Scrapbooks (clippings from Hamilton newspapers and other publications) and Hamilton YWCA SCrapbook.

Terence A. Crowley, Professor of History, University of Guelph. Manuscript of an article, "Madonnas before Magdelenes: Adelaide Hoodless and the Making of the Canadian Gibson Girl." A condensed version of this article to be published in a Canadian history journal early in 1986.

Illustration and Photograph Credits